Now What Am I Teaching Wednesday Night?

Twenty-six More Amazing Bible Stories with Great Applications for Students

by Craig Harris

Illustrated by Janette Coffman

Yikes Again! <u>Now</u> **What Am I Teaching Wednesday Night?**
Copyright © 2000 **Sycamore Tree Publishing Company**

By Craig Harris

All rights reserved. No part of this book, except where indicated for ministry purposes, may be copied without permission from the publisher.

Illustrated by Janette Coffman
Copyright © 2000. Used by Permission
Contact the publisher if you would like more information on Janette

Scripture quotations, unless otherwise indicated, are taken from the *Holy Bible: New International Version.* Copyright © 1973, 1978, 1984 by International Bible Society. Used by permission of Zondervan Publishing House.

Printed in the United States of America   ISBN 0-9663783-1-8

Special Thanks to the editing team who collaborated on this project:
Jodi Harris; Fran Harris; Don Harris; Kevin Harris; Mark Rogers, Master of Divinity, Southwestern Baptist Theological Seminary. Also thanks to Dr. John Ross and Dr. David Squicquero; and to my kids, David and Savannah.

Sycamore Tree Publishing Company
"Climb the Sycamore Tree to see Jesus more clearly"

www.sycamoretreepublishing.com

1-888-627-7848   Fax: 1-419-831-9669

Table of Contents

1. The Snake in the Desert 7
2. The Tower at Siloam 13
3. Zacchaeus Climbs a Sycamore 17
4. Uzzah Touches the Ark 22
5. An Unclean Spirit Returns 27
6. Shimei Curses David 31
7. The Prodigal Son 36
8. Jesus is Tempted 43
9. The Prophetess Deborah 50
10. Jesus Raises Lazarus 56
11. *Jesus Agonizes in the Garden 63
12. The Burning Bush 69
13. *Jesus is Resurrected 75
14. *Mary Magdalene at the Tomb 83
15. Noah Builds an Ark 89
16. Abraham Leaves Home 95
17. A Widow's Offering 102
18. Joshua's Farewell Speech 106
19. Jesus Calms a Storm 112
20. Jesus Heals Ten Lepers 117
21. Elijah and the Baal Prophets 121
22. The Woman at the Well 127
23. Jesus the Twelve-Year-Old 135
24. The Holy Spirit Comes 141
25. *Jesus is Born 149
26. John Writes Revelation 155

*These Stories have seasonal interest.

◼ Introduction:

Student Ministers have the most important job in the world, and one of the busiest. The purpose of this book is to help you prepare meaningful lessons for your students amidst everything else you have to do each week. You will need only about an hour or so to study and prepare for these lessons. Some of the lessons have optional activities that require a small purchase or a small amount of planning ahead, so please begin studying *before* your students arrive for class!

If you study how Jesus taught, you will see that he **told stories**. The Bible calls them parables. Students love to be told stories. Stories, if told correctly, will capture the attention and hold it. Jesus knew how to do this. He would tell stories that his listeners would find relevant to their culture, then use the stories to make applications that he wanted his audience to catch.

This is the idea behind this book: using stories - true stories, straight from the Bible - to teach students the truths that lie within it. The Bible is the most wonderful book ever written, these lessons will help your students learn it and fall in love with it.

How to teach from this book:

1. Study the story from the Bible, then from this book.

We have a paraphrased version of each Bible story. This is only one man's idea of how to tell the story aloud. That is all it is. Read the Bible story first, then read the story in this book to get an idea how to tell it. Then study the actual Bible story some more. When you stand before your students, <u>tell the story in your own words</u>, making sure you stay true to the Biblical account.

2. Take notes on the applications you wish to use.

You may not want to use every application from each lesson. Students learn more when we give them only one, two or three applications and approach them from several angles and teaching styles. You may want to *mention* the other applications, but spend your time on one or two thoughts. Make sure you separate opinion from the Bible. Place each story in context so your students will understand *when* it happened.

3. Have your Bible, this book, and an outline in front of you.

Make an outline of the **Applications** you want to use. As you tell the story, have your outline and an open Bible in front of you. You may wish to have this book in front of you, too, but don't read it - tell it. Highlight selected passages from your Bible that you wish to read directly to your students.

Also, highlight selected passages from this book that you want to make sure you teach.

4. The **Wrap-up** has the basic applications in a nutshell for each story.

5. The **Optional Activity** gives you an activity in which to involve your students each week. Some preparation is usually needed ahead of time for this. These reinforce some aspect of the lesson.

6. The **Teaching Tips** are additional notes to help you teach the lessons with confidence and accuracy. They are found in some sessions.

7. Don't lecture your students for more than twenty minutes at a time.

No matter how good of a speaker you are, you will have difficulty keeping your students' attention for more than about twenty minutes at a time. You begin to lose them after that. Their bodies get tired of sitting and their minds get tired of listening. Practice teaching in twenty minutes or less.

You may want to divide your session time something like this:
1) 20 minutes on singing, registration, announcements.
2) 20 minutes on the Bible story lesson.
3) 20 minutes on the optional activity, skit,s games, video clips, etc.

Change your routine fairly often. This is difficult because we get into comfortable patterns, but let's get *out of the boat* and out of our comfort zones. Our comfort zones can become predictable ruts that bore our students.

8. Use your own ideas and applications.

Please make sure they are Biblically accurate and not based on man's opinion. Make sure your applications align with *all* of the scripture and not just the story at hand. Find modern stories that fit the Scripture - not the other way around. The Power is in the Word of God.

Finally, make sure you keep your students involved each week and teach them to think for themselves.

The Snake in the Desert
Numbers 21: 4-9, John 3: 14

The Israelite people were well into their 40-year trek through the desert. They traveled from Mount Hor along the route to the Red Sea, wanting to go around the land of Edom.

Along the way the people grew impatient and spoke out against God and Moses.

"Why have you brought us out here in the desert to die?" they asked.

"There is no bread, no water - and we detest this miserable manna that we have to eat every day! Life was better in Egypt."

God responded by sending venomous snakes to bite them. Many people were bitten and died. The people came to Moses and said, "We have sinned against you and against God. Pray that the Lord will take the snakes away." So Moses prayed for the people.

God told Moses to construct a replica of a snake and put it up on a pole. Anyone who was bitten and looked at the snake, the Lord said, would be healed and would not die. Moses obeyed and built a bronze snake and raised it on a pole. Anyone who was bitten and looked at it lived.

The Snake in the Desert

Numbers 21: 4 -9, John 3: 14

The Israelite people were well into their 40-year trek through the desert. They traveled from Mount Hor along the route to the Red Sea, wanting to go around the land of Edom.

Along the way the people grew impatient and spoke out against God and Moses.

"Why have you brought us out here in the desert to die?" they asked.

"There is no bread, no water - and we detest this miserable manna that we have to eat every day! Life was better in Egypt."

God responded by sending venomous snakes to bite them. Many people were bitten and died. The people came to Moses and said, "We have sinned against you and against God. Pray that the Lord will take the snakes away." So Moses prayed for the people.

God told Moses to construct a replica of a snake and put it up on a pole. Anyone who was bitten and looked at the snake, the Lord said, would be healed and would not die. Moses obeyed and built a bronze snake and raised it on a pole. Anyone who was bitten and looked at it lived.

1. Trust in God and Live.

There is a simple truth in this story that we find throughout the Bible: We must trust in God. We must trust Him to please Him (**Hebrews 11:6**); we must trust Him for our salvation (**John 3:16**); we must trust Him for everything.

The Israelites didn't trust Him and He let them die in the desert because of it. They didn't trust Him to carry them into the promised land even after seeing His power to free them from Egypt. And now they didn't believe He could sustain them while they were living in the desert. Jesus said those who believe in Him have eternal life, but those who don't are condemned already. (**John 3: 16 - 18**)

This story of the bronze snake makes many Jews uncomfortable according to Bible Scholars. The Lord had recently instructed Moses not to make an image of any animal to worship (**Exodus 20:4**). Why would He instruct Moses to make this image? In truth, though, the people were not to trust in or worship the image of the snake, but in God alone. Ironically, seven hundred years later, King Hezekiah had to tear down the snake because the people had named it "Nehustan" and were worshiping it. (**2 Kings 18:4**)

The entire event makes little sense until we see what Jesus said about it some fifteen hundred years later.

As harsh as this story seems to us today - that our loving God would send snakes among His people to bite them because they grumbled against Him - young people need to know that we must trust in God, or our fate will be worse than being bitten by a snake. Also, the adult Israelites, except Joshua and Caleb, who believed, were going to die in the desert anyway, because God had said so. (**Numbers 14:29 - 35**)

2. Jesus made the story make sense.

Jesus said, in essence, this story was symbolic of his death on the cross. Jesus compared himself to the snake and said, "Just as Moses lifted up the snake in the desert, so the Son of Man must be lifted up, that everyone who believes in Him may have eternal life." (**John 3: 14, 15**)

The Israelites had to trust in God enough to actually look up at the bronze snake for healing of snake bites. It must have seemed strange to them to look at an image of the very thing that bit them to receive healing from it. Why would God ask such a strange thing of them? Jesus said it was because the snake was symbolic of Him. Many scholars believe the bronze snake was on a horizontal beam of a cross - just like the illustration at the beginning of this chapter.

3. We are all snake bitten, spiritually.

We are all snake bitten, spiritually, and Jesus said we must look to Him for healing. *Snake bitten* meaning we are all sinners. (**Romans 3:23**)

Jesus was sinless, so why would He compare himself to a sinful, harmful snake? Paul explains that Jesus *became* sin for us, then was punished -- paying for our sins. (**Galatians 3:13**)

We know from the story of Adam and Eve that the snake is symbolic of Satan and evil. We see from this story in Numbers that God also uses Satan to punish those who don't trust in Him. Jesus didn't become Satan, of course, but He became "cursed" for us. He became sin for us. He took all of the sin and hurting of humanity upon himself on the cross and paid for it all, past, present and future, so that we can have right standing with God. When we *look to* Jesus on the cross, we are admitting that we are sinners and that He paid for that sin. We are stating that we believe in God, we believe in Jesus, and we are trusting in Him for our salvation.

 Wrap-up.

The story of the snake in the desert is a clear picture of what Christ did for us. He was "lifted up" on a cross, just like the snake was lifted up on a pole. Jesus became sin for us on the cross and paid for our sins - if we will trust in Him. Jesus said, "But I, when I am lifted up from the earth, will draw all men to myself." (**John 12:32**) John said Jesus said this to show that he would die on a cross (vs. 33), but Jesus may have had a double meaning here: He surely also meant that if we will lift up His name, He will draw all people who will accept

10

Him into His Kingdom.

This story is another great example of Old Testament scripture that has a direct reference to Christ. Jesus fulfilled more than two hundred prophecies from the Old Testament and can be found in some way in every single book.

If indeed the Jews are uncomfortable with this story, it is because it seems really strange when you take Jesus out of the equation.

Optional Activity.

To illustrate how something can be symbolic of something else, as in this story, make copies of the following page and let the students decipher the cryptic codes. On the sheet, each symbol stands for one and only one letter. Some are filled in to get them started.

Can You Figure Out these Sentences?

Each symbol stands for one and only one letter. Some are filled-in to get you going. The symbols stand for the same letters on every word on the sheet. (✻ is an "E" on every puzzle on this sheet, ▼ is always a "T" but not every "E" and "T" is filled-in for you.)

1. ✻ ✻ ▲ ◆ ▲   ◐ ✻ ☐ ▼
    _ E _ _ _   _ E _ T.

2. ❀ ■ ✻   ◐ ✻ ▼ ✻ ☐ ◆ ▼   ✻ ❁ ✻ ▼ ✻   ✻ ▼
    _ _ D   _ _ _ H _ _ _   _ _ _ _ H   _ _

    ✻ ▲   ✳ ○ ☐ ☐ ▲ ▲ ✻ ❁ ● ✻   ▼ ☐   ☐ ● ✻ ❀ ▲ ✻
    _ S   _ _ P _ S S _ _ L _   _ _   P L _ _ S _

    ✻ ☐ ✻
    _ _ D.

3. ☐ ◆   ○ ◆ ▲ ▼   ❁ ✻   ❁ ☐ ☐ ■   ❀ ✻ ❁ ✻ ■
    Y _ _   _ _ _ _   B _   B O _ _   _ _ _ _ _.

The Tower in Siloam

Luke 13: 1 - 5

A group of people came up and told Jesus about Pilate murdering some Jewish Galileans while they were making a sacrifice to God, mixing their blood with the blood of their sacrifices.

Jesus answered, "Do you think those Galileans were worse sinners than the others because this happened to them? I tell you no! But unless you repent you too will all die. Or those eighteen who died when the tower in Siloam fell on them - do you think they were more guilty than all the other people living in Jerusalem? I tell you no! But unless you repent you too will all perish."

1. God sees things with an eternal perspective.

We see things with an earthly perspective, but God doesn't. He sees the big picture. He knows that our lives on earth are short like "a mist that appears for a little while and then vanishes." (**James 4:14**)

Life on earth is only a finger-snap compared to eternal life. It's not that Jesus didn't care that some lives were lost, He was just much more concerned about their eternal condition than their losing a few short years on earth.

Jesus said in the previous chapter, "I tell you friends, do not be afraid of those who kill the body and after that can do no more. But I will show you whom you should fear: Fear Him who, after the killing of the body, has power to throw you into hell." (**Luke 12: 4,5**)

To kill you is the worse thing someone can do to you. Jesus said not to worry about that. He said, in essence, the most important question is whether or not we are ready to face God. Jesus *did* care about the loss of life, but He had a more important lesson to teach us about death.

2. Long or short life is not necessarily a measure of righteousness.

Jesus was delivered bad news: Some people had been murdered. He then makes reference to an accident that killed others. We live today in an information society - do you ever wonder what Jesus' reaction would be to some of the news we hear today? This passage gives us a clue:

First, Jesus let those around him know that the most important question was if *they* were ready if something like that happened to them.

Next He pointed out that those who were killed were not necessarily "worse sinners" than the others in their area.

God promised the Israelites they would live "long in the land the Lord your

God gives you for all time" if they obeyed His commands (**Deuteronomy 4:40**). It was natural, then, for them to think someone must be a bad "sinner" if his life was cut short. Many of us still think this way today. Jesus said plainly this simply isn't true. We all have to die and God knows how long we will live before we are ever born. (**Psalm 139:16**)

It is true that, in general, we will live a longer, fuller life on earth if we follow God's commands - and the Israelites paid with their lives when they disobeyed God - but many great Christians through the years have lived short lives and it all fits into God's plan. James was murdered by Herod (**Acts 12:2**), but his brother, John, lived to nearly one hundred years, according to church tradition. Both were godly men who loved Jesus with all of their hearts. James died young, in fact, because of his faith. Both men are still "alive" today in Heaven, James just got there first!

You can know for sure that when a younger person dies, that doesn't necessarily mean he was a worse "sinner" than anyone else.

3. Jesus cares about everything about us.

Jesus' answer to the bad news may seem a little insensitive to us today, but we need to remember that the Gospel writers couldn't write everything they heard Jesus say - they had to hit the highlights, under the guidance of the Holy Spirit. We know that Jesus wept (**John 11:35**) when he saw how his friend Martha was hurting over losing her brother. In fact, Jesus told us in **Luke 12:6,7** that God knows when a sparrow dies and He knows how many hairs we have on our heads. He knows everything about us and is concerned about us. Jesus then said not to be afraid because God is watching over us and we are worth more than many sparrows. Yes, God knows that our lives are short and He is most concerned about our eternal condition, but He also cares about everything that happens to us every day of our lives. God is crazy about us and is in ultimate control. Nothing that happens to us is a surprise to Him and He cares very much about us.

 **Wrap-up.**

This amazing story gives us an insight into how Jesus reacted to bad news. He was most concerned about their eternal condition and warned those who were listening that a worse fate awaited them if they didn't turn to God. Jesus also used the situation to explain that long or short life is not necessarily a measure of righteousness, but that all must die and we better all be ready. Jesus does care about everything about us. Nothing happens to us that is a surprise to Him and He is in ultimate control. We must put our trust in Him, turn from our sins and receive His gift of salvation or something worse than being killed will happen to us.

Optional Activity

Before the session, gather newspapers and news magazines. Screen the papers and magazines to make sure all of their content is appropriate for your group. Make sure you have pencils and paper available for each team.

After the lesson, divide your students into teams. Have each team pick a leader. You can pick teams by numbering the students or by having them draw colored strips of paper or different candies from a box. For smaller groups, each person can be a team.

Hand out the papers and magazines to each team. Instruct the students select a story or two and write a short essay on what Jesus' reaction to the stories might be.

Give them ten minutes or so with their teams, then have them come back together and present their essays. Encourage discussion, but be careful to never put down a student for his efforts.

Zacchaeus Climbs a Sycamore
Luke 19: 1 - 10

Jesus was passing through Jericho on his way to Jerusalem where He would be betrayed and crucified. A Jewish man named Zacchaeus was there in Jericho. Zacchaeus was a very rich man, but a crooked tax collector. Tax collectors were hated by the other Jews because their job was to collect taxes for Rome - and they were known for taking much more than Rome demanded and keeping the excess for themselves.

Zacchaeus heard that Jesus was passing through and wanted to see who "this Jesus" was. But Zacchaeus was a short man and could not see over the crowd. (Everywhere Jesus went, crowds would follow Him to see what He would do.) So Zacchaeus ran ahead of where Jesus was and climbed a sycamore-fig tree to get a better view.

When Jesus came to the tree, He looked up and called Zacchaeus by name.

"Zacchaeus, come down now!" He said, "For I must visit you at your house today."

At once, Zacchaeus climbed down and with gladness, received Jesus into his home.

The people of Jericho grumbled about this. "He has gone to be the guest of a sinner," they cried.

Inside, though, something happened to Zacchaeus' heart. He said to Jesus, "Look, Lord! Here and now I give half of my possessions to the poor, and if I have cheated anybody out of anything, I will pay back four times the amount I took."

Jesus said to him, "Today, salvation has come to this man. Zacchaeus is a descendent of Abraham and I came to seek and to save what was lost."

Applications

1. Make an effort to see who Jesus is.

Zacchaeus may have been a crooked man. He may have been hated by his own people because he stole from them to make his living. But Zacchaeus did one thing right: He made an effort to check out who Jesus was. Jesus honored that effort and Zacchaeus is enjoying riches to this day - in heaven!

Jesus was on his way to Jerusalem to be crucified. His earthly ministry was about to end. Zacchaeus had this one shot at gaining his attention and made the best of it. A grown man climbing a sycamore tree may have seemed silly to him and those around him, but he didn't let that stop him. He didn't let anything or anyone stop him from seeing Jesus, and it paid off for him.

Notice the Bible says he wanted to "see who Jesus was," which is more than just seeing *what he looked like* -- Zacchaeus wanted to know what Jesus was all about. If young people will make an effort to see who Jesus is, they won't be disappointed, just like Zacchaeus wasn't.

It is interesting to note, too, that while Zacchaeus was looking for Jesus, Jesus called him by name. If we will only look for Jesus, *He will find us*.

2. Salvation always causes a changed heart.

It wasn't the fact that Zacchaeus gave half of his possessions away and agreed to pay back what he had stolen, with interest, that saved him - faith in Christ is the only thing that saves us. Those things were an outward *result* of that faith. A person cannot earn his salvation, it is a free gift from God (**Ephesians 2:8,9**), but a person who accepts Christ will be different; a new creation (**2 Corinthians 5:17**); born again (**John 3:3**). James says our faith *will* result in action (**James 2:14 - 17**), and that is what happened in Zacchaeus' home that day.

Jesus knew Zacchaeus was born again because he had changed before His eyes.

Zacchaeus' god before he met Jesus was undoubtedly his money. Now, he was giving that 'god' away because he had found the one true God. Money and possessions didn't mean as much to him anymore because he had found the secret to happiness -- a relationship with God, through Jesus.

3. If they call you "shorty", maybe you should be glad.

Zacchaeus may have been put down his whole life - laughed at for being short. But if he had been a tall man, he might have simply stood and watched Jesus walk by. The fact that he was in a tree is what caught Jesus' attention. Think about it: We complain about being different all the time. "I'm too short," "I'm too tall," "I'm too poor," "I'm too fat," "I'm too skinny." God made us just the way we are for a reason. Remember, God doesn't make mistakes and He doesn't make junk. Paul said, "I will boast all the more gladly about my weaknesses, so that Christ's power may rest on me. That is why, for Christ's sake, I delight in weakness, in insults, in hardships, in persecutions, in difficulties. For when I am weak, then I am strong." (**2 Corinthians 12: 9,10**).

The very things that bother us about ourselves may be what we need the most. God makes us like we are, then uses that for our good and His glory.

But Zacchaeus was more than a "shorty", he was also a "sinner". Yes, and Jesus didn't care about either. He went into his home and ate with him. By doing this, Jesus was showing the world that Zacchaeus was His friend. Jesus will accept us, no matter what. He will come into our homes, into our lives, and He will save us if we will let Him.

 **Wrap-up.**

Zacchaeus made an effort to seek Jesus. He overcame what others thought of him and made an actual, physical effort to see Him. He didn't let "the crowd" get in his way.

Jesus called him by name and befriended him. Zacchaeus showed that he was saved by demonstrating a new attitude toward his wealth and possessions. Those possessions never gave him the peace and happiness he was looking for, but Jesus did.

Jesus will use the very things we think are weaknesses for our good if we will let Him.

The Jews were surely offended when Jesus said that Zacchaeus, a child of Abraham, had been saved. They believed their heritage already guaranteed them a spot in heaven. Zacchaeus was saved, though, because he realized he was a sinner and needed Jesus.

Optional Activity.

Have the students prepare and perform a skit, depicting this story. They will need to select the following characters:

- Zacchaeus
- Jesus
- The Crowd
- A tree (?)
- A narrator (optional)
- Zacchaeus' wife (?)

Have them volunteer for the parts, give them 10 or 15 minutes to prepare the skit, then have them perform it for the other students.

4

Uzzah Touches the Ark

1 Chronicles 13: 1 - 14, 15: 11 - 16

David wanted to move the Ark of the Covenant from Kiriath Jearim to Jerusalem. The Ark had been in Kiriath Jearim, ten miles west of Jerusalem, for about one hundred years. It had been stored there since being returned by the Philistines - who had stolen it, but gave it back because God punished them for having it. Saul had neglected it during his reign.

David had already made Jerusalem the political capital of his kingdom and now wanted to make it the center of worship as well. He conferred with his military officers and they all agreed. He assembled as many Israelites from all over the kingdom as he could and went to get the Ark in a loud, worshiping, celebrating procession.

The Ark was at Abinidab's home. David took a new ox cart and placed the Ark upon it. Two men, Ahio and Uzzah guided it as they brought it back. David and the Israelites danced, played instruments and sang praises with all of their might as they walked with it.

When the oxen were walking across a threshing floor in Kidon, they stumbled. Uzzah reached out and touched the Ark, trying to keep it from falling off of the cart. The Lord's anger burned against him and he died on the spot. David became angry at God for striking down Uzzah and named the location "Perez Uzzah", which means "outbreak against Uzzah".

David feared the Lord that day and said, "How can I ever bring the Ark of God to my house?" So David did not take the Ark to Jerusalem, but took it, instead, to the home of Obed-Edom. The Ark stayed there for three months and the Lord blessed Obed-Edom and everything he had.

At the end of the three months, David went again to get the Ark. This time, he consulted the Levite priests. He told them to consecrate themselves and prepare to carry the Ark on their shoulders with poles as the Lord had instructed Moses to move it.

"It was because you Levites did not bring it up the first time that the Lord our God punished us. We did not inquire of Him about how to do it in the prescribed way," he told them.

The Levites hired the best musicians in the land and went to get the Ark. There was much singing, dancing, praising God, and playing of instruments as the Levites carried the Ark to its new resting place, in a permanent tent in Jerusalem.

David, his commanders and elders worshiped the Lord with all of their hearts as the Ark was brought into the city.

Applications

1. God loves us, but we must follow His instructions.

David loved God with all of his heart. His motives were right - he wanted to make Jerusalem the center of worship in his kingdom. He no longer wanted to neglect God's sacred Ark. He wanted to consult God about everything he did. He just made one mistake: He didn't check with God about the proper way to transport the Ark. We have heard so much about God's love for us and how His grace is free to all that we sometimes forget that He is Holy God.

God was very clear about how they were to handle the Ark and other sacred objects. Only the Levites (the priests) were to move the Ark. They were to carry it by running poles through rings on the side of the sacred box. They were not to touch the Ark itself, but only the poles. (**Numbers 4:5 - 15**)

When the Philistines, who were godless pagans, wanted to give the Ark back to Israel a hundred years earlier, God told them through the priests to place it on a new ox cart and let the oxen walk freely back to Israel (**1 Samuel 6:1 - 12**). This was the method David chose when he moved the Ark, but this was not how *Israel* was to move it. David cost a man his life by not following God's instructions. However harsh this sounds to us today, the truth remains: We will die if we don't follow God's instructions, and we may hurt others as well.

"But this isn't fair!," you might say. "Didn't God see Uzzah's heart? Didn't He know he was just trying to keep the Ark from falling? It wasn't his fault anyway, it was David's." All of these arguments sound good, but we must remember that God is God and we must do things His way. God had to show David and all of Israel that *He* was God, *He* was in control and everyone must revere Him.

A lot of good-intentioned, clean-minded, religious people will go to hell because they don't come to God through Christ, which God said is the only way. (**John 14:6**) This may insult our modern "tolerant" mind set, but God is neither modern, nor tolerant. (He *tolerates* - forgives, accepts, loves - us, but He hates and punishes sin and He will only forgive us if we accept His son.)

2. Passionate worship, without proper belief, does not impress God.

Twice in this story David orchestrated passionate, deliberate, emotional worship to God. The first time, the day ended with a worshiper dying. Not until the second time did the Ark arrive safely where David wanted it.

We can worship God with all of our hearts and put all that we have into it, but God only accepts us if we come to Him His way. A lot of people are passionate about their worship, but have not been made right with God because they are trying to come to Him some way other than through Jesus. Perhaps they are trying to earn their salvation, or maybe they are following another religion altogether. God is compassionate and long-suffering, but He will not accept our worship if we do not follow His rules.

David's love for God was evident to all in both cases - with him singing and dancing his heart out before God - but the first try ended badly. David later realized his error and corrected it. In our enthusiasm for God, we must remember His rules.

I'm glad we are given this example of a godly man dancing and singing before God, and I am glad we have this example of instruments being played in worship to God. Sometimes I think we treat church services like God's funeral, not a celebration of the life a living God has given us. This story is a great example of finding the balance between emotional worship and proper attitude toward God's holiness.

 **Wrap-up.**

David cost a man his life because he did not treat God's sacred objects with proper respect. We can have the best of intentions, but must still follow God's rules. Today, we don't have access to the Ark of the Covenant and cannot duplicate the circumstances of this story - but we must give God's *Son* (the new Ark of the Covenant, if you will) proper respect. By this, I mean we must accept Him as our only way of salvation and give our lives to Him.

For us today, this is not a story on the importance of following proper ceremony because Jesus completed that part of the Old Testament. It is a reminder that God must be fully trusted and obeyed or death will result.

Here is a final thought on David's attitude toward Mighty God: Completely trust, obey, respect and give your life to God, then dance, play and sing your heart out before Him in worship!

Optional Activity

Play a game with your students to emphasize the importance of following instructions exactly:

Have your students sit in a circle. (You can use several circles for larger groups - using youth workers as leaders.)

Pick a person in the group. Tell that person that he must repeat a phrase back to you exactly as you say it.

Turn to him and quote something like, "For all have sinned and fall short of the glory of God." But before you say it, clear your throat. See if he can quote it back exactly as you said it - with the throat-clearing and all.

Next, pick another student. Quote "For the wages of sin is death, but the gift of God is eternal life in Christ Jesus our Lord." Wink as you say the word "eternal". The person must wink at the same time you did.

Look at another person, quote "Honor your father and your mother." Scratch your face as you say "father".

See how long you can stump your students before they can repeat back to you *exactly* every time.

Allow your students to try to stump each other if they desire to do so.

Talk to them about the importance of following God's instructions exactly.

An Unclean Spirit Returns
Matthew 12: 43 - 45

Jesus told those around Him this story, "When an unclean spirit comes out of a person, it goes out into desert areas, looking for a restful place, but does not find it. Then it says to itself, 'I will go back to the house where I was.' When it returns, it finds the house unoccupied, swept clean and everything neatly in its place. So it goes and gets seven more spirits, even worse than itself, and they all move into the home. Now, the final condition of the person is worse than before."

Then Jesus said, "This is how it will be with this wicked generation."

1. "Cleaning-up our acts" will never be enough.

Jesus was speaking to very religious people when He told this story. They had emptied their hearts of as much wickedness and sin as they possibly could. They made a genuine effort to be holy, righteous people. They only lacked one thing: While they cleaned their hearts from impurities, they didn't replace those evil desires and habits with anything.

This story is a great example of how religion fails, but how a relationship with God works.

God doesn't want us to have a heart that is empty of impurities - He wants us to have a heart that is full of Him. This is why it is so important for youth leaders to emphasize having a relationship with God more than we emphasize "do's and don'ts". Life is full of rules and regulations - and we saw in the last chapter that we must follow God's commands if we want to live, but *rules without relationship lead to rebellion* and God knows that.

A person who "cleans up his act" had better fill his heart with God's Spirit if he is going to have a chance at keeping his heart clean. The "unclean" spirit in our story (The *NIV* uses the word, "evil" {vs.43}, but a footnote at the bottom of the page explains that in the Greek, the word was better rendered "unclean".) not only returns to live in the newly cleaned house, it also brings seven more even worse spirits with it.

I had a young person come talk to me one afternoon. I had been trying to minister to this young man for years. He had a sweet spirit, but just couldn't seem to get his act together, spiritually. He had been in trouble with the law several times for possessing drugs. He couldn't keep a job and spent all the money he could scrounge on beer and cigarettes. He had dropped out of school.

On this particular afternoon, he came and sat on my patio with me.

"I'm giving up the alcohol and cigarettes," he told me with a big smile. "I'm tired of my life. It's going nowhere. I want to start going to church more and clean up my act."

I thought of this story. I told him bluntly that he never would be able to stay away from drugs and alcohol unless he filled his life with Jesus. He nodded, but didn't answer. To this day, he is still struggling with the same old problems because he never has given his life to Christ. He will stop drinking, smoking and partying for a while, but then he goes right back to it - and worse than before, just like Jesus said he would in this story.

2. Fill your heart with Jesus, then put up a "No Vacancy" sign.

It is true that an idle mind is the devil's workshop. The unclean spirit in our story not only came back to find his old house empty, but also clean and inviting. We have to fill our hearts and minds with *something*. That is the way God made us, and He wants us to fill our hearts with Him. To fill your heart with God means to put Him first in all of your decisions; to love Him most; to *treasure* Him above all other things in your life. The reason the spirit came back in Jesus' illustration was because it couldn't find a place to rest. Perhaps Jesus was saying *we* are restless to find fulfillment. We try to fill the emptiness in our hearts with habits, relationships and material things and always find ourselves needing more because they simply don't satisfy. We have an itch that only God can scratch.

When we fill our hearts with Jesus, we will still make mistakes, we will still sin, but no evil or unclean spirit can *dwell* within us because we have God's power to overcome it. Christians cannot be possessed by an evil spirit and we have the power to overcome habits and temptations that once ruled us.

3. Notice Jesus called the religious people of His day "wicked".

Jesus was making a direct condemnation against the teachers of the law and Pharisees who were listening to Him tell this story. He called them wicked. *They were religious but not righteous.* Only accepting Jesus makes us righteous. Following do's and don'ts will never do it. We can never become good enough to earn God's favor. We can never become good enough to earn heaven on our own. Only by filling our hearts with Jesus can we be reconciled to God. (reconciled means becoming friends again.)

 **Wrap-up.**

Cleaning-up our acts on our own power, without filling our lives with Christ, will never be enough to keep us clean. That just makes our empty lives more inviting to evil. God never called us to live empty lives, but lives filled with His Spirit. If we will let Him, Jesus will come into our hearts, clean up our lives, and fill the vacancy with His love and power. Then we can live victorious lives.

If we try to clean up our acts on our own power, we will eventually end up worse off than ever before.

Optional Activity:

Divide your students into teams of 5 to 10 students. Have them go into separate rooms or areas. Have them elect a spokesperson for each group.

Give each team a sheet of paper with the words:

"Why Can't We Just Say No" on top of it.

Instruct each team to write an essay about this topic on the sheet. Give them about 15 minutes.

Have them come back together and allow the spokespeople to read their group's essays. Let each team have a turn. Allow discussion if you have time.

Shimei Curses David
2 Samuel 16: 5 - 14

David was fleeing from his son Absalom. Absalom was trying to take his father's kingdom by force. When David saw he would have to either run from Jerusalem or fight for it, he ran so he would not be forced to harm his son. He also knew that many residents of his beloved Jerusalem would be killed in the civil battle.

As David, his army, mighty men and supporters who had left Jerusalem with him approached the community of Bahurim, Shimei, son of Gera, appeared on the hillside next to the road they were traveling.

Shimei, from the tribe of Benjamin, was a member of King Saul's family.

He began to scream and curse at David and his officials. He pelted them with rocks and threw dirt on them as they passed by.

"Get out, get out, you worthless scoundrel," he yelled at David, "you are a bloodthirsty man. The Lord has repaid you for the blood you shed in Saul's family, in whose place you have reigned. God has handed your kingdom over to your son Absalom and you have come to ruin because you are a man of blood!"

As it happened, David was flanked on both sides by his armor guard.

One of the men, Abishai, son of Zeruiah, who was David's nephew, said to the king, "Why should we let this dead dog get away with cursing you? Let me go over and cut off his head."

But David said, "I disagree with you Abishai. How do we know the Lord did not tell him to curse me? If my own son is trying to kill me, why not this man from Saul's family? Leave him alone and let him curse. Perhaps the Lord has told him to do it and will repay me with blessings because of the curses I am receiving today."

So David and his men continued down the road with Shimei cursing and throwing rocks and dirt on them along the way.

When the king and all the people arrived at their destination, they were exhausted. But they refreshed themselves there.

1. God says not to repay evil for evil.

Jesus told us not to repay evil for evil. **Matthew 5:39** says *Do not resist an evil person. If someone strikes you on the right cheek, turn to him the other also.* **Matthew 5: 44** says *Love your enemies and pray for those who persecute you.*

It is true that David killed many men, but he was not bloodthirsty. He only killed in battle situations (except for his sin against Bathsheba and Uriah). His very reaction to the curses proved Shimei wrong. David proved by his tolerance that he was a humble man who cared about God and his fellow man. He did not kill out of vengeance.

One of the true marks of a Christian is how well we handle being criticized and put down. Our nature may want us to strike back, but Jesus said not to.

2. How we handle criticism shows our true character.

Every young person is going to have to deal with criticism at some point. Not everyone is going to like you. If you take a stand for God, you may be criticized from within and from outside the church. You will be put down. People will make fun of you. One of the most difficult lessons in life is how to correctly handle someone *cursing at* you. It happened to David; it happened to Jesus. We can count on it happening to us. If we strike back, we are not following God's ideal.

Some criticism doesn't even merit listening to, but *most* criticism can teach us how to be more Christlike if we will listen and heed it. This is true whether the person has our best interests in mind or not. When someone is criticizing you, listen carefully. Throw out what you know is untrue and learn from what just may be.

David's constraint showed his true character. Perhaps one reason David allowed Shimei to curse him was because he knew Shimei was at least partly right. David was innocent of the charges of spilling blood in Saul's family, but maybe he needed to hear that whenever he killed another man, that man's family and friends suffered because of it.

David was wise enough to realize that God could teach him, even through this man's cursings. David said, in essence, "perhaps the Lord will bless me because I am not striking back at this man for abusing me this way."

Later, when David marched triumphantly back into Jerusalem, Shimei came out again and begged for David's forgiveness. David promised him he would not harm him and didn't. (**2 Samuel 19: 18 - 22**.)

3. Shimei's actions eventually caught up with him.

It is interesting to note, though, that the last thing David told his son Solomon, the new king, was to punish Shimei for what he had done. (**1 Kings 2:8,9**) Again, David was not perfect. He kept his word by not harming Shimei himself, but told Solomon to bring him to justice. Solomon, in turn, showed the same constraint he learned from his father. Solomon did eventually have Shimei killed, but only because of Shimei's blatant disobedience to his very generous terms. (**1 Kings 2: 36 - 46**)

David was very Christlike in his tolerance of this abuse, but eventually Shimei's sin caught up with him and cost him his life. That is the way sin is, it always catches up with you. There is always a pay day. Those who curse David's offspring, Jesus - by not accepting Him - will certainly pay. **Romans 6:23** says that payment is death. Cursing a king, then and now, is reckless behavior and punishment is sure to follow.

 **Wrap-up.**

How well we handle criticism shows our true character. It's fairly easy to live like Christ when all is going well. People will eventually interfere with that, though. Some people will not like us and will abuse us, put us down and curse us. David showed by his actions that he was a man of constraint and character. Christ showed the same traits when He was mistreated.

Shimei's actions eventually caught up with him, however, and we must realize that God is not mocked; what we reap, we will sow (**Galatians 6:7**).

Optional Activity:

The words we say can profoundly hurt - or help - each other. Have your students sit in a big circle. Go around the circle, starting with yourself. Have each student give a sincere, true compliment to the person on his right. This cannot be a "veiled putdown" or non-compliment, like "I like your shoes." It must a true compliment like, "I like the way he is always here at church," or "She has a very pretty smile," or "I can always count on him to make me laugh." If time permits, go to the left. If time still permits, have students pick out someone and compliment him. Make sure they don't all pick the same person to compliment.

The Prodigal Son
Luke 15: 11 - 24

Jesus told this story of a father and his two sons:

The younger son said to his father, "Dad, I want you to give me my share of your inheritance right now - I don't want to wait until you die."

His father, wanting to please him, did as he asked and gave him a large sum of money.

Not long after that, the son took his money and went off to live in another country and wasted it on wild living. Soon, the money was all gone. A severe famine set in and the son began to be hungry and in need. So, he went to work for a man who raised pigs. For a Jew, this was the most insulting job imaginable. He would feed the pigs their slop every day and was so hungry, the pig food began to look good to him. But his friends were gone and no one would help him.

When he came to his senses, he said to himself, "My father's servants have plenty of food and here I am starving to death. I will go home and admit to my father that I have sinned against God and him. I'll tell him that I am no longer worthy to be called his son and I will ask him to hire me as one of his servants."

He then got up and headed home.

While he was still a long way from home, his father saw him and was filled with compassion for him; he ran out to his son, threw his arms around him and kissed him.

"Father," the son started his speech, "I have sinned against God and against you. I am no longer worthy to be called your son..."

But the father interrupted him and called to his servants, "Quick! Bring the best robe and put it on him, put a ring on his finger and sandals on his feet. Go get the fatted calf and prepare it. Let's have a feast and celebrate, for this son of mine was dead and is alive again; he was lost and is found." So they began to celebrate.

Applications

1. God is always waiting for us to come home.

"We all like sheep have gone astray." (**Isaiah 53:6**) This story is a wonderful picture of a loving father waiting for his errant child to come home. It is a beautiful picture of God giving us salvation if we will only "come home" to Him.

The son took advantage of his father's goodness and grace and went and blew his father's riches on sinful living. But the father didn't hold grudges, but instead missed his son and longed for him to come home. We know this because Jesus says in the story that the father saw him "while he was still a long way off." This is a clear picture of a man sitting on his porch watching for his son to return.

God is watching for our return to Him. When we come to our senses and make an effort to go to Him, He will see us coming and run out to meet us.

The father in the story didn't even punish his son. Perhaps the son had been through enough and he knew it; instead he rejoiced in seeing him and celebrated. **Luke 15:10** says there is much rejoicing in heaven when one sinner repents and turns to God. God forgives and forgets. (**Psalm 103:12**)

2. There are always consequences to our actions.

As we said, the father didn't punish his son when he came home, instead he celebrated. But the son's inheritance was spent and would have to be built up again. God completely forgives us when we sin, but He allows us to suffer the full consequences of our actions. (**Galatians 6:7,8**) The son nearly starved before he came to his senses, but as we see in the story, that suffering sent him right where he belonged. God lets us suffer the consequences of our actions, then often uses that suffering to get our attention and change our behavior.

3. The Father offers full pardon and sonship.

The father in the story told his servants to put the best robe on him, a ring on his finger and sandals on his feet. These are very symbolic: The robe stands for honor. (Remember Joseph's robe? **Genesis 37:3**) God *clothes* us in Jesus' righteousness - his honor. The ring symbolized authority. It gave him the "power of attorney", where the son could make decisions concerning the household. The sandals distinguished him from slaves. Children had shoes and slaves didn't. God accepts us as children, even though we don't deserve it. The son had apparently lost his shoes somewhere along the way and was living like a slave - a slave to his own sin, but now he was given sonship. Sonship and the freedom that that implies. This is how God treats us, like honored sons and daughters.

4. We must go to God with a proper attitude.

Notice, though, that when the son returned home he told his father that he had sinned against him and against God. He was prepared to tell him that he was no longer worthy to be called his son. He was going to ask him if he would just hire him as a servant. But the father would not let him finish. The father saw the proper attitude and knew in his heart he could begin to celebrate.

When we "come home" to God, we need to approach Him as unworthy servants. We need to be sorry for our sin and repent of it.

 Wrap-up.

This story is a beautiful picture of our loving, heavenly Father waiting patiently for us to come to our senses and return home to Him. He will see us coming and run to meet us. He will completely forgive us and give us a place of honor, authority and sonship in his kingdom. He loves us and does not want to lose any of us. If we haven't "come home" to Him yet, we need to look around and see that we are living like slaves in a pigpen while He offers everything we need for life and happiness.

Please note when you are teaching this, that salvation only happens once in a person's life. This story is not teaching about a "saved" person who is coming back to salvation after losing it - it is teaching about a "lost" person who is being "found" for the first (and only) time (see verse 32). The Bible teaches that our salvation is secure. (John 3:16, John 10:29, Romans 8:1**)

Optional Activity:

Prayerfully consider giving an invitation (to accept Christ as Savior) to your students following this lesson. Ask them to close their eyes and bow their heads - so that they can block out all distractions. In your own words, ask them this question:

"If you died tonight and were standing in front of God and He asked you why He should let you into his heaven, what would you say?"

As they think about their answers, tell them that the Bible teaches that the only way to come to God is through faith in Jesus.

Have them repeat the following prayer outloud (Have every student repeat this, whether they are already Christians or not.)

      Dear God   (repeat)
      I thank you that you sent Jesus to die for me.   (repeat)
      I believe the Jesus died for me and rose from the dead on
         the third day.   (repeat)
      I admit that I am a sinner and I cannot save myself. (repeat)
      I ask you now to forgive me of my sins. (repeat)
      Please come into my heart and save me. (repeat)
      And I promise that from today on, I will try to live for you.
                        (repeat)
      Amen. (repeat)

Now ask them to look up at you. Ask if anyone just prayed that prayer for the first time and meant it. Have them either raise their hands or stand to their feet if so. Have a mature student, a student worker, or you yourself go and counsel with any who indicate they have just asked Jesus to save them.

Show them that the prayer they prayed was based on the following scriptures: **Romans 3:23, Romans 5:8, Romans 6:23, Romans 10:9,10 and John 3:16.** (Please memorize these scriptures if you haven't already done so and encourage your students to do the same.)

Let them know that when they ask Jesus to save them, He promises that He **will** (**Romans 10:13**), let them know that Jesus holds onto them and they don't have to ever worry about Him letting them go - He won't. (**John 10:29**)

Now they need to be baptized, join a local church, read their Bibles, pray all day every day, and hang out with other Christians who will encourage their new walk.

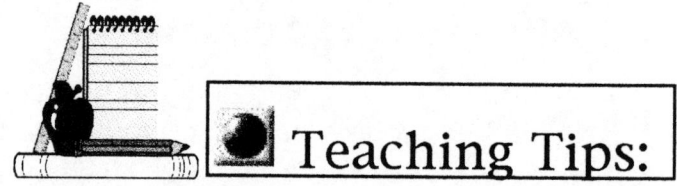 **Teaching Tips:**

    Of course, Jesus' story does not end with the son coming home and being restored. He then tells about the older brother who stayed true to his father and is jealous of his brother's treatment. We didn't go into that part of it for simplicity's sake. Some say that *that* part of the story is the real meat of the parable because it deals with the Jewish nation being jealous of Gentiles coming into the Kingdom of God. It is also a lesson for the Christian Church today because it symbolizes our not wanting "sinners" to come into the church family.

    This part of the story is another great lesson perhaps for another day.

Jesus is Tempted

Matthew 4: 1 - 11

The Spirit of God led Jesus into the desert to be tempted. Jesus went without food for 40 days and was understandably hungry. Satan came up to him and said, "If you are the Son of God, tell these stones to become bread."

Jesus answered him, "It is written: 'Man does not live by bread alone, but on every word that comes from the mouth of God.'"

Then the devil took Jesus to Jerusalem and had him stand on the highest point of the temple. "If you are really the Son of God," he said, "throw yourself down. For it is written: 'He will command his angels concerning you, and they will lift you up in their hands, so that you will not strike your foot against a stone.'"

Jesus answered him, "It is also written: 'Do not put the Lord your God to the test.'"

Next, Satan took him to a very high mountain and showed him all the kingdoms of the world and their splendor. "All this I will give you," he said, "if you will bow down and worship me."

Jesus said to him, "Away from me Satan! For it is written: 'Worship the Lord your God, and serve him only.'"

Then the devil left and angels came and ministered to Him.

1. Like Jesus, we will all be tempted.

If Jesus himself was tempted, we can count on being tempted, too. Young people need to realize that Satan is a real person - he is not some symbolic force - he is a fallen angel, God's enemy, and he really is out to get us. The Bible teaches that Jesus was tempted in all the basic ways we are today and He didn't give in to a single temptation (**Hebrews 4:15**). We, on the other hand, have all given in (**Romans 3:23**).

Only by following Jesus' example and becoming more and more like Him will we overcome temptations. There are several things we can learn from this story about how to be victorious when we are tempted.

2. Jesus was tempted when He was weak and hungry, but spiritually high.

Satan came and tempted Jesus at a vulnerable moment. Satan does not play fair. He will lie to us, cheat us, or destroy us if we aren't on our guard and wearing our armor (**John 10:10, Ephesians 6:11, 1 Peter 5:8**).

Satan will attack when we are least prepared. Make no mistake, he is the type of guy who will kick you when you are down. Jesus had recently been on the spiritual high of His baptism (**Matthew 3:13 - 17**) and was hungry and thirsty from a 40-day fast. Young people can expect an attack from Satan when they return from a spiritual camp or retreat, and after they have made a major commitment to Christ.

The devil also attacks us at our weak points. Jesus was hungry, so the first temptation was to use His powers to make food to eat. That must have been a real temptation for Jesus and Satan knew it. But we will see in a moment how Jesus overcame it.

Teenagers are especially vulnerable in several areas: First, they crave acceptance and popularity; second, their bodies are maturing and they are discovering the opposite sex; third, they are experiencing more freedom of decisions than ever before. So, these are the areas where Satan will attack them.

3. Satan uses the same temptations on us that he used on Jesus.

I have heard it said that Satan only tempts us in four ways: power, pleasure, fame and fortune. That's how he tempted Eve in the garden, that's how he tempted Jesus in the desert, and that's how he tempts us.

Let's see what Jesus' temptations were: First, to turn stones into bread. *What would have been so wrong with Jesus using his powers to turn stones into bread and eating them?* He would have broken his fast early, which was a commitment to God. Satan loves for us to break our vows to God, but God hates that. He would have also had to use His powers for his own *pleasure*, and not for God's work. If Jesus was going to experience life as a man, he had to refrain from twitching his nose like *Bewitched* to make life easier for Himself.

Second, Satan tempted Jesus to use God's power to save Him from His own actions. God wants us to live by faith, not by magical signs. The Bible teaches that we will reap what we sow (**Galatians 6:7**). If we jump off of a building, we will kill or maim ourselves. God does protect us within His will, but we do not have the right to break His laws and rules and expect Him to bail us out. Again, the temptation for Jesus here was to use God's power for His own purposes.

The third temptation was for power, pleasure, fame *and* fortune! Satan was tempting Jesus to set up an earthly kingdom and rule over it. This was what the Jews expected the Messiah to do and must have been a real temptation for Jesus. *Wouldn't a throne have been better than a cross?* Wouldn't the adoration of everyone have been better than rejection, stripes, nails and death? Wouldn't it have been easier to live in a palace with riches than walk the dusty streets without a home? But Jesus knew what His mission was and resisted the temptation to change it.

Most young people are tempted by popularity, pleasure and material possessions. These are all okay so long as we are putting God and His desires first in our lives; so long as we are not breaking His laws to gain them,; and so long as the delight of our hearts is God and not those things (**Psalm 37:4**).

4. We defeat temptations the same way Jesus did.

Jesus used the scripture to answer Satan. Jesus didn't try to reason with him or bargain with him. He knew the scripture and made it His offense against the devil. Paul said in **Ephesians 6:17** that our only offensive weapon against the devil is the Word of God.

Put simply, the only way we can defeat Satan and resist his temptations is by knowing and doing the Word of God. Young people will never be able to resist temptations until they commit the Word of God to their hearts and lives (**Psalm 119:11**).

Jesus had only the Old Testament Scripture to quote when He walked the earth, and that's what He used. Today, we have the gift of the Old and New Testaments and both are good for battle. Young people can and must memorize scripture and do what it says if they are to have any hope at all of defeating Satan's temptations.

It is good to remember, too, that Jesus defeated Satan after spending 40 days in prayer. This is not a coincidence. Jesus spent hours in prayer. That is our other offense against Satan and temptation -- large doses of prayer. After Paul lists the Armor of God in **Ephesians 6**, he caps it by saying to pray all the time. (Verses 18 - 20. He uses a form of the word "prayer" five times in three verses in the NIV.)

 **Wrap-up.**

Jesus was tempted in the same basic ways we are: power, pleasure, fame and fortune. Jesus was able to defeat the temptations because He knew the scripture and He knew what God wanted from Him and was committed to doing it.

Young people must know the scripture if they are going to defeat Satan's temptations. They also need to spend plenty of time in prayer. That's what Jesus did.

Optional Activity:

If young people are going to defeat temptation, they are going to have to learn and memorize scripture. Divide your students into teams of 3 to 5, depending on the size of your group. Have each team go into a different room or area. As they go to their areas, give each team a scripture passage to memorize from the following list:

John 10:10; Romans 3:23; Romans 6:23; Mark 12:30, 31; Galatians 2:20; Ephesians 2:8,9; Psalm 37:4; Revelation 3:16

Give them 10 to 15 minutes, depending on how much time you have, to memorize their team's verse. Instruct each team member to memorize their team's verse.

Have them come back together and take turns quoting their verses. Give a prize to the teams who can all say their verses.

Remind your students that it is important to memorize the *address* of a scripture (where it is), too, so they can put it in its proper context.

Teaching Tips:

It is important to remember that it is not a sin to be tempted. Jesus was tempted in this story, but was without sin. *We can't help it if birds fly over our heads, but we don't have to let them nest in our hair.* The problem begins when we dwell on the temptation, then act on it (**James 1:13 - 15**).

In this story, the Bible says the Holy Spirit led Jesus into the desert to be tempted. God's plan was for Jesus to be tempted, just like we are, and to show us that He could defeat it. By implication, then, so can we. Jesus was no doubt continually tempted, just like we are, but this story gave us the basic temptations He faced. As we saw, they are our same basic temptations too.

I have heard it said that since **Hebrews 4:15** says, "we have one who was tempted in every way, just as we are -- yet was without sin," that means Jesus was tempted to become a homosexual or even a pedophile, since He had to be tempted in *every* way we humans are. That's nonsense. Jesus was simply tempted in the four basic ways we are tempted, not in every single temptation people face. We can be certain that Jesus was never tempted to speed in a car.

We mentioned earlier that Jesus spent large amounts of time in prayer. It wasn't just prayer here, though, it was also fasting. Fasting means going without food and sometimes liquids as we devote time to prayer. Have you ever fasted? Have your students? You will find it a very fulfilling experience, if not. (Most fasts are only for a couple of days.)

Can a person go without food for 40 days? Yes, it has been done many times by many people. You cannot go that many days without water, and Jesus apparently did not.

Is there really a mountain where you can see all of the kingdoms of the earth? No, Satan may have taken Him to a high mountain where Jesus could imagine all of the world's kingdoms, or see a representative part of the major kingdoms of that day. Or, it could have been a supernatural event. The point is that Jesus' temptation was to be an earthly king, like His friends and family wanted Him to.

To keep the lesson simple, I did not elaborate on the scriptures Jesus used to rebut Satan, but they are: **Deuteronomy 8:3, Deuteronomy 6:16,** and **Deuteronomy 6:13.**

Notice that Satan used a scripture (**Psalm 91:11, 12**) to tempt Jesus to do wrong. This shows how clever he is. Satan is not a creator, only a perverter, and will even use scripture - taken out of context - to persuade us to do wrong. This is a clear example of the importance of learning good, sound doctrine.

The word in the Greek for "tempt" in this passage is more accurately rendered "test". God allows us to be tested to show us that we can win and to make us stronger. God does not tempt, but He does test us (**James 1:13**).

9

The Prophetess Deborah
Judges 4 & 5

Deborah, the wife of Lappidoth, was the fourth and only female judge in Israel and one of five women in the Old Testament who was called a prophetess. She would sit under a palm tree, "The Palm of Deborah" and hold court for the Israelite people. People would come to her to let her settle their disputes and give advice. She was so well respected, she earned the title "a mother in Israel".

One day, she called one of Israel's generals, Barak, to her and said, "the Lord, the God of Israel commands you: Go, take ten thousand soldiers to Mount Tabor. I, the Lord, will lure your enemy Sisera and his troops to the Kishon River and give him into your hands."

Sisera was the commander of King Jabin's army. Jabin was a Canaanite king who had been oppressing the Israelites for twenty years. His army had nine hundred iron chariots and would terrorize the Israelite people, killing and stealing from them. The Lord had allowed this because the Israelite people had done evil in His sight. Now, they cried out to Him and He was about to answer.

Barak said to her, "I will only go if you will go with me. If you will not go with me, then I will not go."

"Very well," Deborah said, "I will go with you. But because you refuse to go without me, the honor of victory will not be yours. The Lord will hand Sisera over to a woman to be killed by her."

So Deborah went with Barak up to Mount Tabor, along with ten thousand men.

When Sisera heard that Barak was at Mount Tabor, he gathered his men and their nine hundred iron chariots and advanced toward his position.

When Sisera made it to the Kishon River, Deborah said to Barak, "Go! This is the day the Lord has given Sisera into your hands. The Lord has gone ahead of you, so go now!

Barak advanced, and the Lord routed Sisera's army at the Kishon River. Sisera, however, abandoned his chariot and fled on foot. Meanwhile, Barak's army pursued Sisera's army all the way back to Harosheth Haggoyim, where it had been stationed. Barak's troops killed all of Sisera's men; none was left.

Sisera ran to the tent of Heber, a man who had sided with him. When he arrived at the tent, Heber's wife, Jael, met him. "Come inside," she said, "and do not be afraid."

He went into the tent and asked for water, but she gave him milk instead and covered him with a blanket to hide him. He commanded her not to tell anyone he was there and, exhausted, soon fell asleep.

When he was asleep, she took a tent peg and a hammer and drove the peg through his temple and into the ground, killing him instantly.

Soon Barak came to the tent looking for Sisera and Jael showed him his body.

On that day God subdued Jabin, the Canaanite king, and eventually Israel completely destroyed him.

1. God can use women just as easily as He can men for his plans.

Chalk one up for women everywhere! God used a woman in this story to bring glory to His name -- in fact, He used *two* women.

Deborah (pronounced DEB' oh ruh) was an honored judge, leader and prophetess (female prophet). From all indications, she was the very leader of the country. (This was before Israel anointed kings...about 1200 years before Christ.) This was a society that didn't allow women to speak in public, much less run the country, and yet that is what she did.)

It may be that no man had enough faith to be the leader, or more likely, she was simply an extraordinary woman and the power of God was upon her. She was wise in her judgments, respected by the men of the society, and most important, listened to God. We see by this story that God used her to speak for Him.

If God could use Deborah this way in the Old Testament, He certainly can use women today. There may be girls in your youth group who want to serve God but are afraid to because they are female. This story should encourage every girl that God can use them, too. It won't be easy - women are usually paid less and have to work harder for respect, but I believe girls can step up to the task and serve God with the best of them.

[The Bible teaches that men should lead in *worship* services in **I Corinthians 14:34**, but notice **I Corinthians 11:5** implies that women *can* pray aloud and speak in church services. Paul may have been writing about a specific problem at Corinth in light of the culture of the day. This matter has been the subject of much debate., but I think this story of Deborah is proof that God can use women in a mighty way.]

So, women have to find ways to serve God like Deborah did. True, there is no biblical precedent for women to be an *elder* or *senior pastor*, but we find deaconesses, leaders of countries, judges, prayer warriors, prophetesses, missionaries, financial supporters and other godly women in the Bible. Some were leaders and some worked behind the scenes, but all were vitally important in the Kingdom of God.

God uses us in our weaknesses and here He used the "weaker sex" to provide strong leadership and win mighty victories for Israel, a job normally reserved for men only.

No matter what "society" thinks of you, God sees you as an overwhelming conqueror! (**Romans 8:37**)

2. God is not afraid of the things we are.

This story has some of the greatest military strategy in history and it was God, through Deborah, who planned it. Barak and his ten thousand troops were stationed on a hill - which gave them an immediate advantage. But they didn't stay there as you might expect. God told them to charge down the hill and meet the enemy at the river. Why? It is strongly implied here that Sisera's chariots either became mired in the mud or bogged down in the crossing of the river. (See **Judges 5:20, 21**). Twice in the narrative the nine hundred iron chariots are mentioned although the number of Sisera's troops is never given. Obviously, it was the chariots that gave them their military advantage and struck fear in the hearts of the Israelites. But God used that very strength against them! Having to cross the Kishon River was their weakness and Barak's men took full advantage of it.

It is good to remember that the things we fear do not frighten God. He will use the strengths of our adversaries against them for His glory and our good.

Barak may have wanted to stay on the hill and let the enemy attack him there. But because he was obedient to God, he had victory that day. Sisera probably would have simply overrun his position and slaughtered his troops had he stayed on the hill. He had victory because he obeyed and charged ahead.

We will have victory in our lives if we will obey and charge ahead.

3. Fear costs us honor.

Barak could have been the most celebrated man of his day. He could have been the hero of this story. Parents might name their sons "Barak" to this day (maybe it is a good thing he is not the hero!) -- if he had simply obeyed God's command and led his troops into battle like Deborah instructed him.

But he is not the hero in this story because he lacked the faith to go without Deborah. She saw this and prophesied that a woman would take Sisera's life and steal the honor of victory from him. (When you first read this, you think she was referring to herself, but as the story progresses we see that she was referring to Jael, who killed Sisera.)

Why wouldn't Barak go without Deborah? Clearly he saw that God was with her. He trusted her judgment and he wanted to make sure God went with him on the campaign. In other words, he knew that God would be there directing the battle plan if Deborah went.

We don't need any other mediator between God and ourselves. We have Christ and He is all we need. God will give us all of the "battle plans" we need to live victorious lives through His Word. When, in our fear, we put another mediator between ourselves and God, we are costing ourselves the honor that faith in Him alone could bring. In fact, Jesus told us not to place any other mediator between God and ourselves. He said He was the "gate of the sheep pen" (**John 10:7**) and the "only way to the Father" (**John 14:6**). This goes for our prayer life as well as our salvation.

 **Wrap-up.**

God wants and deserves the glory for His achievements. Here is a story where a mighty military victory is won -- and Israel is saved from oppression from a godless king -- and God received all of the credit. God always deserves the credit for anything good in our lives.

Deborah was faithful and obedient to Him. She was well respected and honored although she was a woman in a culture that did not celebrate women's rights or equality.

God is not afraid of the things we fear. He is God and has everything under His control. If we will just obey and trust Him, we will receive honor for doing so. God will, in fact, use the very strengths of his adversaries against them to prove His power.

Optional Activity:

Divide your students into teams of 3 to 10, depending on the size of your group. You can do this by having them "count off" if you wish. Tell them to elect a <u>girl</u> as a team leader in each group.

Have each team go into a separate room or area. Give each team a scripture passage from the list below and have them write a report on how the woman (or women) in the story made a difference in the Kingdom of God with her life:

Matthew 1:18 - 25, 2 Timothy 1:3 - 7, Acts 18, Esther 7, 2 Kings 4:1 - 7

The teams will need pens, paper and a Bible to complete their tasks.

Give each team 10 minutes to prepare their reports.

Have the teams come back together and have the leaders of each group read and present their team's report to the rest of the group, in turn.

If you have another Bible story you wish for them to use, feel free to do so. I avoided **Ruth** here because of the length of the story.

10

Jesus Raises Lazarus
John 11: 1 - 44

A man named Lazarus was very sick. He was from Bethany and was Mary and Martha's brother. Jesus was very close to Lazarus and his sisters. Mary, in fact, was the one who once poured perfume on Jesus' feet and wiped them with her hair. The sisters sent word to Jesus, who was preaching miles away, across the Jordan River, telling Him that Lazarus was sick. When Jesus heard this, He told His disciples that this sickness would not end in death. "It is for God's glory so that God's Son may be glorified through it," He told them.

It is true that Jesus loved Lazarus and Mary and Martha, but He deliberately stayed where He was for two more days before He began His journey to Bethany.

Then He broke the news to the disciples that He wished to go back to Judea -- where Bethany was. This sounded dangerous to the disciples because they knew that Bethany was near Jerusalem where the Jews had tried to stone Jesus the last time they were there.

Jesus assured them that He was in His Father's will and they would be walking in God's light and protection when they returned.

He then told the disciples that Lazarus had fallen asleep and He was going to awaken him. The disciples didn't understand why Jesus would have to do that, so Jesus explained to them clearly that Lazarus was dead.

"I am glad I was not there to heal him so that you may believe," He told them. "Let's go to him now."

When Jesus came near the town, He was told that Lazarus had been in the tomb for four days. Bethany was only two miles from Jerusalem and many Jews had come from there to comfort the sisters.

Martha heard that Jesus was on his way and went out to meet Him, while Mary stayed at home.

"Lord," Martha said to Him, "If only you had been here earlier, my brother would not have died. But I know even now God will give you whatever you ask."

"Your brother will live again." Jesus assured her.

"I know he will rise again in the resurrection at the last day," Martha said to Him.

"I am the resurrection -- and the life," Jesus said, "He who believes in me will never die. Do you believe this?"

"Yes," she said, "I believe you are the Christ, the Son of God."

At this, Martha went back home and told Mary that Jesus was nearby and was asking for her.

Mary went out to where He was and fell at His feet. "Lord, if you had been here, my brother would not have died," she said.

Several of the Jews had followed Mary to Jesus. Jesus saw Mary crying and the Jews with her crying as well and was deeply moved.

"Where have you buried him?" Jesus asked her.

"Come and see," she answered. Jesus wept.

The Jews saw this and said "See how He loved him." Others said, "He could open the eyes of a blind man, so why couldn't He keep this man from dying?"

Jesus was deeply moved when He arrived at the cave where Lazarus was buried. There was a large stone laid across the entrance.

"Take away the stone," Jesus told them.

"But Lord," Mary said, "he has been dead for four days now and there will be an odor."

"Remember," Jesus told her, "I told you that if you believe, you will see the glory of God."

So they took away the stone. Jesus looked up to heaven and prayed to the Father, "Father, I thank you you that you have heard me. I know this, of course, but I am saying this for the benefit of these who are listening."

Then He called out in a loud voice, "Lazarus, come out!"

Lazarus came out, his hands and feet wrapped with strips of linen, and a cloth around his face.

Jesus said to them, "Take off his grave clothes and let him go."

Applications

1. With Jesus, there is always hope.

Mary and Martha both felt that Jesus could have healed Lazarus if he had still been alive. But Jesus deliberately stayed away until Lazarus died so He could show them God's true power. Jesus has power even over death. Death was the one thing that ended all of our hope, but not anymore. Now that we know Christ, our hope continues even after all other hope is gone.

Martha knew that she had the hope of seeing Lazarus again "in the resurrection", in other words, when Jesus returns the second time, but Jesus explained to her that since He *was* the resurrection, she didn't have to wait any longer. Now that Jesus has conquered death, we can go immediately to Heaven and do not have to wait until "the last day" to have eternal life.

Jesus stole Lazarus from the grip of death long after all hope was gone and He can give us life again, too, if it is God's will. Scores of Christians through the ages have been given the news that they have terminal cancer, but then God miraculously intervened. A youth-speaker friend of mine, Scott Crenshaw, told me once how robbers stole his car then shot him twice in the back of the head from point-blank range as he lay on the ground, but he walked away with only a scratch on his shoulder from a third bullet. He heard the gun fire, he felt the steel of the barrel on the back of his head, but nothing happened. Since that day he has led many many young people to Christ. God simply wasn't through with him yet. With Jesus, there is always hope.

2. Lazarus wasn't free to go until his friends removed his grave clothes.

When Lazarus appeared from the cave he had been interred in, he was bound by the clothes of a dead person: strips of cloth binding his hands, feet and head. Jesus told those around him to loose the cloths from him and let him go. We can learn a couple of things here. First, as my friend Scott has told my students, we are not truly free to live the new life in Christ until we remove our graves clothes. Scott says grave clothes are things in our lives that are associated with our "old selves". Things that lost and "dead" people do. Things that we once did that do not please the heart of God. Things to which we cling instead of trusting in God. Many students have new life in Christ, but do not live the full abundant life they could because they are trying to walk in their new life wearing their old grave clothes. Grave clothes restrict our lives and they reek with the smell of death.

But notice that Lazarus couldn't get out of those mummifying cloths on his own. His hands were bound and he needed the help of his friends and family to get free. The same remains true today: We need each other to help us become free of the "old life" and to become free in Christ. Jesus does all of the real work, but He relies on us to help each other reach our fullest potential.

Being accountable to one another is one of the most important ways we can remain true to our commitments to God. We need the strength and encouragement of our friends to remain faithful and to live a life free of the old "clothes" that once kept us from being free.

3. Jesus wept.

This is the shortest verse in the Bible. Many of us memorized it because it *is* so short - almost as a joke - but this verse speaks volumes about Jesus. Why did He cry? He knew He was about to raise Lazarus from the dead and stop the sisters' suffering. He knew that God was about to demonstrate His incredible power. He knew He was about to see Lazarus again, alive and well. So why did He weep?

I think this short but powerful verse tells us that Jesus really does care about us and really does feel our suffering when we are in pain. **Hebrews 4:15** says Jesus understands and sympathizes with us and this story proves that this is true. Jesus was hurting for His friends. He loved them and did not want to see them suffer. He knew that He had caused them temporary pain by delaying His coming and He felt their agony. He knew that God's plan was the most important thing He could do, and it was therefore necessary to allow Lazarus to die so He could demonstrate God's true power, but Jesus wept because His friends wept. Jesus hurt because His friends were in pain. Jesus cried because He was overcome with real, human emotion.

Yes, have your students memorize this verse; not because it is short, but because it tells us very much about our compassionate and caring Savior.

 **Wrap-up.**

With Jesus, we always have hope. Jesus takes our fear out of life and can even take the fear out of death. Jesus has power over death. We have the assurance of eternal life and of never having to taste death when we believe in Christ.

We do, however, have to remove those things from our past that may be keeping us from living a free, abundant life. Young people need to hold each other accountable in the removing of those "grave clothes" that may be keeping them from being free to live as God would have them.

One thing we can know for sure from this story is that Jesus truly cares about us and weeps with us when we suffer.

Optional Activity:

Have your student bow their heads and close their eyes. Encourage them to think of things in their lives that might be "grave clothes" that are keeping them from living the free, abundant life that God offers.

Pass out strips of paper and pens or pencils and have the students write down things that may be "grave clothes" on them. Instruct them not to look at anyone else's paper. Provide a trash can for them to throw the strips into if you wish, or have them take the strips home to further pray about them.

Pray aloud with them over these commitments.

If you have time, ask the students if they would like to share with the group a "grave clothing" that they need help overcoming. Be sensitive and keep the session appropriate, but see where the Spirit may lead.

Other students may want to volunteer to hold their peers accountable to commitments with which they are struggling.

11

Jesus Agonizes in the Garden
Mark 14: 32 - 42

Jesus had just eaten the Last Supper with his disciples and would soon be arrested and crucified. He knew this full well and was in agony because of it. Jesus did not want to experience the *excruciating* pain of the cross, or the beating He would take beforehand, or the pain of death, or the unbearable weight of the sins of the world or the abandonment of His friends during the process.

Now He went to a familiar place. Each evening, while He and the disciples were staying in Jerusalem during Passover week, He would take them out to an olive garden called Gethsemane to pray.

He told eight of the disciples to stay at a place and pray. He then took His three closest friends, Peter, James and John, a little further into the grove.

"My soul is overwhelmed to the point of death," Jesus told them.

They could see that He was deeply distressed and troubled. He then told the three of them to watch and pray while He walked a little further still.

There, He fell to the ground and prayed, "Abba, Father, everything is possible for you. Take this cup from me. But not what I will, but what you will."

When He returned to His disciples, He found them sleeping. "Simon," He said to Peter, "are you asleep? Could you not keep watch for one hour? Watch and pray so that you will not fall into temptation. The spirit is willing, but the body is weak."

Once more He went away and prayed the same thing. Upon returning, He found them sleeping again, for they were exhausted.

A third time, He went and prayed and was in anguish. He was in such distress and sweating so profusely that the sweat drops were mingled with blood.

Returning a third time, He again found the disciples asleep.

"Are you still sleeping and resting?" He asked them. "Enough! The hour has come for the Son of Man to be betrayed into the hands of sinners. Get up! Let's go! Here comes my betrayer!"

Applications

1. Jesus went to a familiar place to pray.

Luke 21:37 tells us that Jesus went to Gethsemane to pray each evening while He was staying in Jerusalem that week. **Matthew 24:2** talks about Jesus sitting in this same garden during the day and teaching there. Then, when Jesus was deeply distressed about the coming events, He retreated to His comfortable spot to spend time alone with God.

We need to have a comfortable place where we can get away from the distractions and spend time each day with God. If Jesus needed this, how much more do we?

Once, our seven-month-old daughter was facing surgery to repair her aorta. It was pretty serious, as you can imagine. One day, the doctor called me at my office at the church and told me that there was a chance, although small, that she could be paralyzed by the surgery. Those words struck fear in me to the very core of my being. I slumped up the stairs to the youth room where I had taught many lessons about God being with us and how His power can conquer any challenge we face. I spent an hour there weeping, praying and crying out to God. But I was in a comfortable spot. I was in a place where I had read God's word over and over about how He will never leave or forsake us. I was in a place where I had seen God do mighty things in people's lives. I couldn't think of a better place to be at that time. I drew comfort just from being there. Our daughter, Savannah, came out of the surgery fine. Praise be to God for comfortable places to pray.

When Jesus taught His disciples about prayer in **Matthew 6:6**, He told them, "Go into your room, close the door and pray to your Father." Young people may be tempted to listen to music or have the TV on during their quiet times, but these things are a distraction. They may even want to meet with others for their prayer times. Of course that is good to a point, but we need to spend time *alone* with God each day so we can build our *own* relationship with Him. This is what He desires. *Be still and know that I am God.* (**Psalm 46:10**)

2. Jesus took His friends along - to a point.

Jesus took eight of the disciples with Him and had them sit on the hillside. Then He took His three closest friends a little further. When He prayed, though, He went away from all of them and spent that time alone with the Father.

This is a good picture of our different levels of friends being with us in difficult times. There are those friends that we want nearby, praying for us. Maybe this represents our church family or extended biological family. Then, we want our closest friends *very* near - so that we can draw strength from their presence.

Today, it is important that we have true friends who will pray for us and sit with us during difficult situations. The disciples did not fare too well - they mostly slept - but at least they were nearby and that is what matters most in times of trouble, grieving and distress.

Students need to have true friends who will sit with them and pray for them, but they also must *be* true friends who will do that for their friends in return.

But notice, though, that the actual praying was done alone. That was between Jesus and the Father. This is a good example of a great prayer warrior. Jesus spent many hours during His life on earth in secret prayer with the Father.

3. Jesus was determined to do His Father's will.

It is important to note how deeply distressed Jesus was in this story. This was no easy task before Him and He did not want to go through the agony and torture He was facing. He soon would be beaten, whipped, spit upon, mocked, abandoned, forced to wear a crown of thorns, and nailed to a cross to die. He was facing the very sting of death.

More horrible than that, though, He soon would bear the weight of the sins of the whole world. All of my sin and all of yours. He, the Holy One, would soon become sin for us and punish that sin in His body to satisfy God's anger toward it. **(Colossians 1:21, 22)**

The famous picture of Jesus serenely kneeling by a rock and praying does not really show the true picture of what happened. Matthew and Mark both tell us that He "fell on the ground" and prayed. Luke adds that Jesus' sweat fell "like drops of blood". This may mean the sweat drops were so large they resembled blood drops, or more likely, that blood was mingled with the sweat because He was sweating so profusely. His pores had opened to the point that blood escaped through them.

Jesus was in agony because He desperately wanted not to go through with this, but we can see clearly that He was totally determined to do so anyway. He was determined to do God's will no matter what the consequences to Him personally were.

When was the last time you fell on the ground and sweat drops of blood because you were so determined to do God's will, even though you desperately didn't want to?

Here in America, we have a religion of convenience. We love the gospel and the grace of God, but when things get tough and there is a sacrifice involved, we back off and say, "That goes against my rights!" Jesus gave up His rights in the garden. Jesus was not an American and all of us who are saved should probably be glad about that.

The disciples acted more like us Americans. They slept through the whole thing because they were tired. Yes, and because of their lack of discipline and prayer, they soon abandoned Jesus when He really needed them. Their spirits may have been willing, but they failed because their bodies were weak and undisciplined and they were not connecting with the Father to receive the strength they needed.

 **Wrap-up.**

Jesus was deeply distressed and in agony in the garden, "to the point of death," He said. He went to a familiar place to pray and took His friends with Him. But when it came time to pray, He spent time alone with the Father.

Jesus shows us how much He wanted not to go through the torture, agony and pain He was about to face. But He desired most of all to do His Father's will and was determined to do so.

He only asked His friends to stay awake and pray with Him that He would have to strength to endure and they would have the strength to stand with Him, but they could not stay awake. Here, as in many cases, Jesus had no one to rely upon except the Father. The Father responded by sending an angel (**Luke 22:43**) to comfort Him, but Jesus still had to do His Father's will and die for us.

Optional Activity:

To emphasize the importance of praying for each other:

Have your students write on strips of paper prayer needs that they have right now.

Encourage them to share with the other students those needs if they wish, making sure the needs spoken are appropriate for your group.

(Be careful here that they do not disclose concerns and requests that are *too* hurtful about themselves or their families. You also might want to make sure they don't begin to *brag* about how bad they are or what they have done.)

Have the students sit in a chair, one at a time, and have the other students surround them and pray for them. Have the praying students lay hands on them if you feel it is appropriate for your group. Have at least one student or worker pray aloud for each student who has come to the chair.

Remind your students that they are not to gossip to anyone about the concerns that are mentioned in this session.

Reemphasize to your students the importance of praying for one another and of "being there" for each other in times of trouble and need.

The Burning Bush

Exodus 3: 1 - 14

Moses was tending the flock of his father-in-law, Jethro. Jethro was a priest of the Midianites. Moses led the sheep to the far side of the desert and came to Horeb, the mountain of God.

Suddenly, he saw a bush that was burning, but was not consumed by the fire. Moses wondered what might be causing such a thing and walked over for a closer look. When God saw that Moses had come close to the the bush, He called out to him from inside of it, "Moses! Moses!"

Moses said, "Here I am."

"Do not come any closer," God said to him. "Take off your sandals for you are standing on Holy ground."

Then God said, "I am the God of your father, the God of Abraham, the God of Isaac and the God of Jacob."

Moses hid his face, afraid to look at God.

"I have indeed seen the misery of my people in Egypt. I have heard their crying out because of their slave drivers, and I am concerned about their suffering. So I have come down to rescue them from the hand of the Egyptians and to bring them out of the land and into a good and spacious land, a land flowing with milk and honey - the home of the Canaanites, Hittites, Amorites, Perizzites, Hivites and Jebusites.

"The cry of the Israelites has reached me and I have seen the way the Egyptians have mistreated them. So now go. I am sending you to Pharaoh to bring my people out of Egypt."

Moses said, "But who am I, that I should go to Pharaoh and bring the Israelites out of Egypt?"

So God said, "I will be with you. And this will be a sign to you that it is I who have sent you: when you have brought the people out of Egypt, you will worship God on this mountain."

"But suppose I go to the Israelites," Moses said, "and say to them, 'The God of your fathers has sent me to you,' and they ask me, 'What is his name?' What shall I tell them?"

"I AM WHO I AM," God said. "Tell the Israelites that 'I AM' has sent you."

Applications

1. Any old bush will do!

Did you notice that the Bible does not tell us what kind of bush it was that Moses saw burning? Maybe that's because it doesn't matter. The power of the flame and the instructions that came from within were from God, not the bush. So, any old bush would have done just fine.

God's power doesn't depend on what class of person we are today. He can use the rich and poor, young and old, tall and short - whomever - alike. It doesn't matter to Him because He is *I AM*, not us. We are merely His instruments for His use.

2. God didn't speak until He had Moses' attention.

I think a lot of young people want to hear from God, but they are too busy to listen to Him. *God is not going to yell above the noise in our lives.* If we want to hear what He has to say, we need to step away from what we are doing and give Him our full attention.

Moses had seen fire before. He had probably seen bushes burn before. But what was special here was that this bush didn't burn up. He knew there was something different going on. After he approached the bush to investigate and God knew He had Moses' full attention, *then* He spoke and forever changed history. When we see that the power of God is not going away and we give Him our full attention, then He will speak and reveal His will to us. Not before.

We mentioned in the last session that Jesus withdrew to a quiet place alone to hear from God. Moses did the same thing here. He dropped what he was doing to investigate a miraculous sight. God has given us the 'burning bush' called the Bible, and we need to drop everything to get close to it and hear what it says to us.

3. God demands proper respect.

It is also important to note that God told Moses to take off his sandals. When we approach Almighty God, we need to do so with reverence and proper respect. *Teenagers should not expect God to speak to them while they are living a disrespectful lifestyle.* If young people want to hear from God, they will have to treat their parents with proper respect, honor God with their bodies, and avoid filling their minds with garbage.

I am not asking you to impose a legalistic lifestyle upon your students, I am simply pointing out that God demands proper respect - and that comes from the heart (**Colossians 2:20 - 23**).

4. "Tell them that I AM sent you."

Many of your students probably have plaques on their bedroom doors that explain the meaning of their names. Back in **Exodus 3**, about thirty-four hundred years ago, a person's name meant much more than it does today.

Back then, a person's name told you something about him. It was meant to disclose what his character was. It was very important to them to have a good name because their name carried all of the power of the person.

When Moses asked God in whose name he would be representing, he was telling God that he needed His name because if he had God's name, he had the *authority* that went with it. It is interesting to remember that God had not revealed His name up until this time. But now He was revealing Himself to mankind. Now, He was about to give us His laws and show us what He expects from us.

God told Moses that He was the God of the past: "I am the God of your fathers - the God of Abraham, Isaac and Jacob." He said He was the God of the present: "I have seen the way the Egyptians are oppressing them." And He is the God of the future: "I am sending you to Pharaoh..."

God's name says it all. He is the I AM. He is eternal; the God of the past, present and future. He is all in all and all that. He is it. He is everything. His name says that He is almighty, all powerful, all knowing God. His name says there cannot be any higher authority than Himself.

Young people can accomplish everything God wants them to when they live in His name. If I try to do something in *my* name, I may fail. But if I will go forward in God's name, I can accomplish everything He wants me to (**Philippians 4:13**).

 **Wrap-up.**

God has great plans for all of us, just as He did for Moses. But we must give Him our full attention and proper respect if we expect to hear from Him. We may not see a burning bush, but we have the miracle of the Bible as God's witness today. If we will obey God and go forth in His name, we can accomplish mighty things, just like Moses did.

Also, God can use all of us if He chooses. It doesn't matter who we are or what we look like, what matters is if we are available to Him. God doesn't need our abilities, He simply needs our availability.

Optional Activity:

In advance, purchase some pipe cleaners, popsicle sticks, drinking straws, glue and rubber bands from your local Walmart-type store.

Divide your students into teams of 4 to 10 people, depending on the size of your group.

Tell them to select a leader for their teams.

Throw each team a handful of the pipe-cleaners and straws or popsicle sticks. Provide them with glue and rubber bands.

Tell them they have 10 minutes to make something with their supplies.

If you wish, you can have them make something from Moses' life - like his water basket, the burning bush, a chariot, or a figure of Moses himself.

Or, you may allow them, if you prefer, to make anything they want - but they will need to keep it appropriate and explain it to the rest of the group later.

When the ten minutes have passed, have all of the teams come back together. Have a spokesperson from each team show and explain what they made. Make sure each team member participates in some way.

Jesus is Resurrected

Luke 24: 1 - 12

Early on the first day of the week, Mary Magdalene, Joanna, Jesus' mother, Mary, and other women went to the tomb to anoint Jesus' body with spices they had prepared. When they arrived, they found the stone rolled away from the entrance of the tomb. They went inside but did not find Jesus' body. They were wondering what this could mean when suddenly two men in white appeared and stood beside them. The men's clothing glowed like lightning. The women were terrified and bowed to the ground before them.

"Why do you look for the living among the dead?" one of the men asked them. "He is not here; He is risen! Remember how He told you, when He was still in Galilee: 'The Son of Man must be delivered into the hands of sinful men, be crucified and on the third day be raised again.'"

Then the women remembered that Jesus had told them all of this.

When they came back from the tomb, they told the others what had happened. The disciples did not believe them, though, for their words made no sense to them. Peter, however, got up and ran to the tomb. Bending down to enter in, he saw the strips of linen lying by themselves. He went away, marveling at what had happened.

1. If Jesus is not risen, then our faith is useless.

The whole Gospel message stands or falls on the truth of this incident. If Jesus really came back from the dead, then He was indeed the Son of God. If He was the Son of God, then we can have eternal life, God's promises are true, our prayers are being heard and answered, and our life has meaning. If He came back from the dead, then He is Lord of all and was not just a liar.

If someone stole Jesus' body, as some claim, then our faith is useless and we are dead in our sins (**1 Corinthians 15:14**). If Jesus did not rise again, then we have no hope of life after death. We have no hope of ever seeing our loved ones again. We have no hope of our prayers being heard or answered. We have no hope of our life having any meaning or purpose. Life itself has no meaning. Wow! How sad!

But Jesus *did* rise again from the dead! The evidence is overwhelming. (Please see chart on page 79.)

2. Jesus conquered death when He rose again.

We hear a lot about Jesus dying on the cross for us - and indeed it is very important that we fully understand that, but He didn't stay dead! When Jesus rose from the dead, He conquered our most feared enemy. He defeated death. If He can overcome death itself, then He can defeat any other problem, challenge or difficulty we may ever have. When He defeated death, He proved once and for all that He is God and has all of the power in the universe at His disposal. There is nothing we should ever fear, now that we know that Jesus triumphed over sin and death.

3. Since Jesus *is* life, we can have life to it's fullest today.

1 John 5:12 says "He who has the Son has life; he who does not have the Son does not have life." In **John 11: 25**, Jesus said, "I am the resurrection and the life. He who believes in me will live, even though he dies." The second half of **John 10:10** says, "I have come that they may have life, and have it to the full." Notice in these scriptures, Jesus offers us life *now*, not just after we die. It is a sad mistake to think we will only enjoy our Christian lives after we die and arrive in heaven. Our life in Christ begins at the moment of our salvation. We can live abundant, full lives in Christ *today*. We don't have to wait until tomorrow or until our death to begin truly living. The life Jesus gives us is in the *present tense*; it is life today and tomorrow and forever.

There is a restaurant, Joe's Crab Shack, that has a big sign out front that says "Free crabs tomorrow". I love this sign because no matter when you go in to eat it is always *today* and never tomorrow. In that sense, tomorrow never comes! If we are waiting until tomorrow to begin living our lives, tomorrow will never come and we will never begin to live. Live life today. Jesus has given it to us. By faith in Him, we can live life to its fullest *right now*.

 **Wrap-up.**

If Jesus rose from the dead, then He proved that He was who He said He was. If He did not rise again, then our faith is useless and we are dead in our sins, we have no hope for life after death or for meaning in this life.

Since Jesus conquered death, we can live an abundant life today, all of God's promises are true and our prayers are being heard.

Since history has proven that Jesus rose from the dead, we must make sure we tell everyone that He is the only way to heaven, since that is what He claimed. We must accept *all* of the Bible, including God's claims for our lives, if we accept the great news about His conquering death and hell for us.

Optional Activity:

Make a copy of the "Ten Proofs that Jesus Rose from the Dead" found on the following pages for each of your students.

Divide the students into teams and have each team study and discuss one or more of the proofs, then have them report to the other students.

You can divide the students by numbering them. Have the teams select team leaders. Give each team one or more proofs, depending on the size of your group. Give the teams 10 to 15 minutes to study their assignments. When time has expired, have the teams come back together to give their reports to the other students.

Encourage your students to take the essays home and discuss them with their parents and friends.

Ten Proofs that Jesus Rose from the Dead

1. The Bible says He did.
   The Bible is the most amazing, miraculous book ever written.
   a. We have more than five thousand Greek manuscripts dating back to within one hundred years of the autographs (hand-written letters).
   b. In the Gospel accounts, Jesus fulfills more than 450 Old Testament prophecies about the Messiah.[1]
   c. No other religious book has internal prophesies that came true. The Bible was written by 40 authors on three continents in three languages over fourteen-hundred years. Yet the authors all agree with each other.

2. The reports of the empty tomb.
   a. Women first reported His disappearance and women were not considered legal witnesses in that day. If this was a "made-up" story, there is no way the authors would have women finding the tomb first.
   b. The disciples were not expecting the tomb to be empty and had no preconceived notions about it.
   c. There were soldiers there guarding the tomb to make sure no one stole His body.

3. The multiple appearances to many witnesses after the resurrection.
   a. The Bible records that more than 500 people saw Jesus after the crucifixion (**I Corinthians 15:6**). There is no way this many people could have had the same hallucination. Any person who knew Jesus' body had been stolen could have come forward and stopped the church before it began.

4. The conversion of skeptics, doubters and non-believers.
   a. Thomas would not believe Jesus arose until he saw and beheld him.
   b. Jesus' brother James was not a believer until after he saw Jesus after the resurrection.
   c. Paul was a staunch Jew until he encountered the risen Christ.
   d. Many skeptics today put their faith in Christ after they see the evidence. Hundreds give their lives to Christ everyday to this day.

5. Archeological evidence.
   Archeologists are finding more and more physical evidence from the ancient world that prove the accuracy of the scripture. Just some

examples:
- a. A rock with Pontious Pilate's name on it was found in 1961.[2]
- b. A rock with the inscription "House of David" was found in 1993.[3]
- c. Quirinius Caesar's coins have been found.[4]

6. The fact that Jesus forever changed History.
- a. When we write today's date, we are acknowledging Christ's birth.
- b. An estimated ten thousand Jews left their beloved belief system to follow Christ. Many died for their new faith. There are still millions of Jews in the world today, but none of the other Old Testament peoples still exist. This shows how important their heritage is to them, and yet many have left it to follow Christ.[5]
- c. The Christians were a small band of criminals in the eyes of the Roman Empire, but by 300 A.D., Rome had become a Christian nation. (We name our children Peter and Paul and our dogs Caesar and Nero.)

7. The early practice of Communion and Baptism.
- a. Communion would not have been practiced in the early church if Jesus' death didn't mean anything, and the only way it means anything is if He came back from the dead.[6]
- b. Baptism changed its meaning from "the washing of sin" (**Mark 1:4**) to become symbolic of the death, burial and resurrection of Christ. (**Romans 6:3,4**)

8. The fact that the "cowardly" disciples died for what they saw.
- a. The eleven disciples ran scared the night Jesus was arrested. Peter denied even knowing Him. But, after seeing Jesus raised from the dead, history tells us they became evangelists who all died except John, who was exiled on an island, for their beliefs.
- b. There is an important difference in dying for your beliefs and dying for what you saw. You may die for something you sincerely believe, but will you die for something you *know* is *not* true? The disciples wouldn't have either. They would have had nothing to gain for lying about the resurrection, but plenty to lose.[7]

9. The emergence and growth of the church.

The church has not only grown at an incredible speed, but has done so under intense persecution. The church would have died in infancy if someone could have proven that Jesus did not rise again. Many people *wanted* to stop the church but could not because they could not produce His body.

10. The ongoing encounters with Christ today.

Millions of people from all nations, cultures and walks of life have accepted Christ and continue to accept Him as Savior. All of us who have done so know in our hearts and minds that Jesus Christ is indeed alive today because, for one thing, His Holy Spirit tells us so (**Romans 8:16**).

Notes

1. Grant R Jeffrey, *Jesus, The Great Debate*, Frontier Research Publications, page 191.
2. Randall Price, *The Stones Cry Out*, Harvest House Publishing, page 308.
3. Ibid., page 167.
4. Ibid., page 299.
5. Lee Strobel, *The Case For Christ*, Zondervan Publishing House, page 340.
6. Ibid., page 341.
7. Josh McDowell, *The New Evidence That Demands a Verdict*, Nelson Publishing, page 271.

Permission is granted to copy this essay and use it for ministry purposes.

14

Mary Magdalene at the Tomb

John 20: 10 - 18

Peter and John had just seen the empty tomb and had returned to where they were staying. Mary Magdalene, who had told them that the tomb was empty, stayed behind at its entrance. She stood there, weeping. She wept with confusion about what had happened and she wept with sadness over losing such a wonderful friend. Jesus had cast seven demons from her and she had shown her appreciation by supporting Him financially.

As she wept, she stooped and looked once again inside the tomb where Jesus had been. When she did, she saw two angels, one at the head and one at the feet of where Jesus had been.

"Woman, why are you crying?" they asked her.

"Someone has taken my Lord away," she told them, "and I don't know where they have put him."

Suddenly, when she turned around, Jesus was standing behind her, but she did not recognize Him.

"Woman," He said, "why are you crying? Who are you looking for?"

"Sir," she replied, thinking He was the caretaker of the garden, "if you have taken His body, please tell me where you have put Him and I will go get Him."

Jesus said to her, "Mary."

When He said her name, she recognized Him and cried out in Aramaic, "Rabboni!" which means teacher.

But Jesus said to her, "Please don't cling to me, I have not yet ascended to my Father. Go to my brothers and tell them that I am returning to my Father and your Father and my God and your God."

Mary went with joy to the disciples and told them, "I have seen the Lord!" She told them what she had seen and what Jesus had said to her.

Applications

1. Mary didn't recognize who Jesus was.

Why didn't Mary Magdalene recognize Jesus? She was a close friend, disciple and follower. He had healed her of a spiritual condition and she had supported Him financially during His ministry (**Luke 8:1 - 3**).

It may be that she couldn't see well in the early morning light, especially through her tears. She also was obviously not expecting to see Him alive. You can look right at something that is before you, but that you are not expecting, and your mind may not compute or accept it. Also, Jesus may have looked somewhat different than when she had last seen Him. He was in His new body - the body that could eat (**John 21:15**), but could suddenly appear in a locked room (**John 20:19**). The answer is probably a combination of all of these factors.

Mary was expecting to mourn and cry for a long time over losing Jesus. She was in a sad fog and was not seeing clearly. Her mind was not equipped to see Him alive again - that was beyond her dreams and expectations. She simply wanted to know where His body was so she could give it a proper burial and mourn over it.

But Jesus was alive! No one had taken His body, He was alive again! Jesus had conquered death and had proven that He was who He claimed to be.

Suddenly, her mourning had turned into joy and her life would never be the same again. *When we encounter the risen Lord, our lives are never the same again.* Mary was looking for a living Savior among the dead. He was not there and He still isn't! I'm glad we celebrate a living Lord and don't memorialize a dead hero.

Even in our most sad and frightening moments, Jesus is there. We may not always recognize Him because of our own frailties and lack of faith, but He is there. As we shall see, though, it didn't matter whether Mary recognized Jesus, what mattered was that He recognized her.

2. Jesus recognized Mary.

The important thing was not whether or not Mary Magdalene recognized Jesus; what was important was that Jesus recognized *her*. Someday, when I stand face to face with God, it won't matter if I recognize Him - what will matter is whether or not He recognizes me!

Jesus said many will say to Him on the last day, "Lord, Lord, did we not prophesy in your name, and in your name drive out demons and perform many miracles?" but He will say to them, "I never knew you. Away from me, you evildoers!" (**Matthew 7:22, 23**). In verse 21, Jesus had just said that the way to heaven is by "doing the will of the Father." Clearly, "works" won't save you, because those Jesus mentioned here were preaching and performing miracles. So what is "the will of my Father" Jesus is speaking about? In **John 6:29**, Jesus says, "the work of God is this: to believe in the One He has sent."

The only way God can truly know us is if we believe in Jesus and accept Him as Savior.

Jesus knew Mary Magdalene because she believed in Him and put her trust in Him. She didn't understand the significance of the empty tomb yet, but she believed that Jesus was the Messiah. Faith in Jesus is our one and only hope.

Some might say, "but aren't we all God's children? Doesn't He know all of us by name?" True, God calls each of us by name to salvation, but most people reject His call and therefore do not belong to Him. They have no promise from God that He will hear their prayers or have a personal relationship with them. God knows everyone's name, but not everyone *belongs* to Him. This is apparently what Jesus was referring to in **Matthew 7**. Everyone is God's creation, but not everyone is His child (**Romans 8:15,16**) and His friend (**John 15:15**). There is a big, big difference and eternity is at stake.

3. Jesus called Mary Magdalene by name.

Mary didn't recognize Jesus until He called her by name. God knows how important it is to us to be recognized by our names. She was not just some woman standing at the tomb, she was His friend. When we belong to Jesus, He says we are His friends (**John 15:15**). Friends know each other's names. Mary recognized Jesus when He called her name because she had heard Him say her name many times before. Jesus said in **John 10: 1 -10** that He calls his sheep by name and they know His voice.

I remember my own salvation experience as a seven-year-old child. I was sitting in church and felt as though God was "calling" me to come to Him. I didn't feel like God was calling everyone in the service that day, just me. It was a very personal thing between God and me. That's what salvation is all about: God calls us individually - by name.

And God still knows my name. He has called me His child, His friend and His masterpiece (**Ephesians 2:10**), and I continue to have a personal relationship with Him to this day.

 **Wrap-up.**

In times of trouble or suffering, we may not recognize that Jesus is standing nearby, but He is. She was clearly disappointed with God and disillusioned with her faith, but instead of being a defeat for Christ - and her, this was a great victory. He is a risen Savior and is alive and well today. Can you see God's hand in all circumstances, good or bad?

He knows us and calls us by name if we belong to Him. He knew Mary Magdalene because she trusted in Him. Mary had the privilege of being the first person to see Jesus after He rose from the dead.

God calls everyone by name to salvation, but few accept His free gift. When a person rejects this gift, Jesus is forced to tell him that He never knew him, in other words, that the person does not belong to Him. Does God know you?

Optional Activity:

To emphasize the importance of having our names known, play a **name game** with your students:

Have the students sit in a circle. Ask the first person, the person on your right, to say his name and a food item that starts with the same letter as his name.

Some examples: "My name is Ray and I like raisins"
                 "My name is Donna and I like donuts"
                 "My name is Amber and I like apples"

The next person says his own name and food association and then the first person's and so on. As you go around the circle, the students will have to remember more and more students' names and food associations.

You go last and say them all.

Emphasize to your students that God loves them all and calls them all by name to accept and love Him.

Noah Builds the Ark

Genesis 6 - 9

The world had become a vile place. People had forgotten about God and were sinning against Him. So, God declared that He was going to destroy every person and creature on it in one hundred and twenty years and wipe the slate clean.

But Noah was a righteous man, blameless among the people. He walked with God and found favor in His eyes. So, God spared Noah and his family.

God told Noah to construct a huge floating box - an ark. God was very specific about the dimensions and materials to be used to build the ark. It was to be 450 feet long, 75 feet wide and 45 feet high. It had separate rooms and compartments on three levels and was made watertight with tar. God told Noah to take two of every kind of animal that breathes into the ark with him. He further told Noah to take seven pairs of "clean" animals for sacrifice to God and seven pairs of every kind of bird.

God told Noah that He was about to flood to earth and destroy every person and animal upon it - except for Noah and his family and the animals they would take with them into the ark.

Noah did all that God told him to do.

When the one hundred and twenty years had ended, He told Noah to take his sons, gather the animals and enter the ark.

"Seven days from now I will send rain on the earth for forty days and nights, and I will wipe from the surface of the earth every living creature I have made."

So Noah and his wife and his three sons and their wives entered the ark. The animals came to Noah and entered too, and God shut the door behind them. Then the rain began to fall. Noah was 600 years old when the rain began. Water rushed up from underground and the floodgates of heaven were opened. The rain fell for forty days and forty nights.

The water covered the whole earth for six months. The water was twenty feet over the highest mountain peaks. Then it began to reside. The ark rested in the mountains of Ararat, but it was another forty days before Noah could see any dry land. Then, after they had been in the ark for more than a year, God told Noah to leave the ark and repopulate the earth.

Noah built an altar to God and worshiped Him. God made a covenant with Noah that He would never flood the earth again and said the rainbow would be a reminder of that promise.

Applications

1. Noah was different than everyone else.

The first thing we have to understand about this story is that Noah was a righteous man in a world full of evil and corrupt people. In fact, the Bible says he *walked with God.* This is the very thing God wants from us (**Micah 6:8**). This means we have a relationship - a friendship - with Him. Noah did and it saved him and his family.

He was probably not popular because of his stand for God. He was different and different people are not usually liked, but that is what God has called us to be. Everyone around us may ignore or even hate God, but we must walk with God in holiness and righteousness. (The word *holy* means "set apart".)

Walking with God has never been easy in this fallen world, but it will save you from destruction.

This story shows how seriously God takes sin: He *will* judge sin, and everyone who rejects Him will pay with their lives and their souls.

2. Noah obeyed God even though it may have seemed silly at the time.

Five times in this story, the Bible says that Noah obeyed what God told him to do (**Genesis 6:22; 7:5, 9, 16; 8:17, 18**). This is one of the most important aspects of this story - the fact that Noah obeyed God. In fact, the writer of Hebrews mentions this (**Hebrews 11:7**) to emphasize Noah's faith in an event that was more than a hundred years away.

A hundred years away? Yes, based on verse 6:3, we see that God decided to flood the earth in 120 years. Noah must have taken most of that time to build such a huge structure. I can imagine people making fun of Noah the whole time he built this huge floating box. But Noah's obedience was a long-term commitment. I can see some Christians today beginning the project, but abandoning it after a year or two. Not Noah; he finished what he started and worked hard to make it happen.

This project must have really looked foolish to those who saw it; a man working night and day to build a mammoth structure like this. We don't know where Noah lived, but even if he built it near the ocean, he could have never gotten it into the water!

> The ark did not look like a boat as we know them. It was literally a floating box. It was as long as one and a half football fields and as tall as a four-story building. Scholars and scientists have studied its dimensions and say it could have held nearly 45,000 animals (which is more than there were...), with room for food, water and provision for all of them for a year. Shipbuilders use its same length-to-width ratio, 6 to 1, to this day.

Noah undoubtedly had to put up with laughter and ridicule for the entire one hundred and twenty years. He probably had his sons to help him, but perhaps no one else.

Also, Noah would have had to work his other job, probably farming, to feed himself and his family while he built the ark. This whole project called for hard work. That brings us to our next point:

3. Noah needed God's help to accomplish this task.

How did he get those huge timbers to the ark and into place? How did he get all of those animals into the ark and keep them separate so they wouldn't eat each other?* How did he keep them from eating him!? What did Noah tell his wife and sons during the one hundred and twenty years he worked on the ark? Obviously, he couldn't have done this without God's help.

That's when God has us right where He wants us: when we cannot accomplish what He wants without Him. And, like Noah, we cannot please God without faith (**Hebrews 11:6**).

We can see from this story how faith and obedience go hand in hand: Noah would not have obeyed God unless he had faith in Him, and his obedience ultimately strengthened his faith.

*This was a supernatural event. The Bible says the animals *came* to the ark (vs. 7:9) in pairs. God picked them and told them to go and they obeyed. If God can create an animal, He can surely tell it where to go and how to act when it gets there. In fact, this whole story tells of a supernatural event. There is no way we can believe this really happened without faith, but we must believe it because the Bible says it is true.

This story tells us plainly that God's tasks are not always easy. Usually, we have to sacrifice and work hard to do God's will. But with God's help, we can do all things He wants us to (**Philippians 4:13**). Jesus also promised that "my yoke is easy and my burden is light" when we work for Him (**Matthew 11:28 - 30**). In other words, we *can* do God's will if we will do it in His strength and power.

 **Wrap-up.**

This is an incredible story of a man who stood out from the crowd. Noah walked with God and was a righteous man when all those around him lived in contempt for God. Because Noah found favor in God's eyes, he was spared when God flooded the planet, destroying all other men and land animals.

Noah obeyed God, even when it may have seemed silly or hard to do. He worked hard for more than one hundred years to accomplish the task God set before him. He was a great man of faith, endurance, courage and commitment.

God is looking for young people today who are like Noah. Do yours stand out from the crowd? Do they walk with God when those around them don't? Will they obey God no matter what He tells them to do? Will they stick to the tasks set before them? If not, disaster may be waiting.

Optional Activity:

Get a big pot or wash tub out of your church's kitchen. If you can't find one, get one from home. Fill it about three-quarter's full with water. Purchase some *Lifesavers* candy.

After the lesson, divide your students into teams of 4 to 10, depending on the size of your group. Have the teams elect a leader.

Give each team some popsicle sticks, scotch tape and drinking straws. (You should have these supplies left over if you did the optional activity from lesson 12 in this book.)

Tell each team to make a floating "ark" with their supplies. Tell them that their boat must float with your keys on top of it for 10 seconds.

Give them ten minutes or so to build their arks.

Have them come back together after the ten minutes and take turns floating their creations.

Award the winning teams with rolls of *Lifesavers* candy.

Abraham Leaves Home

Genesis; 12 - 21

Abram, later known as Abraham, lived in the city of Ur in the land of the Chaldeans. God spoke to Abraham and told him to leave his country, his people and his family and go to a new place. God told Abraham that He would show him where to live once he arrived.

The Lord told Abraham that He would make him into a great nation and would bless him; He told Abraham He would make his name great and that Abraham would be a blessing.

"I will bless those who bless you," God said, "and whoever curses you I will curse; and all the peoples of the earth will be blessed through you."

Abraham obeyed. He took his father, Terah; his wife, Sarai (later God named her Sarah); his nephew, Lot, and with them, set out to the new land. The group traveled up the Euphrates River to a community called Haran and stopped there. It was there that Abraham's father, Terah, died. Then Abraham, Sarah and Lot continued south to the land of Canaan, where they stopped at a place called Shechem.

Abraham was seventy-five years old when he left Haran. He and his wife, Sarah, were not able to have children. She was sixty-five when they left for Canaan.

At Shechem, the Lord appeared to Abraham and told him that He was going to give this land to his offspring. Abraham built an altar and worshiped the Lord there. Then he continued south and pitched his tent in the hills east of Bethel, near Jerusalem (called Salem at that time).

Soon, however, there was a famine in the land. Abraham and his enclave traveled through the Negev desert to Egypt, where there was plenty of food.

*Later, Abraham took Sarah and Lot and all of their possessions and traveled through the Negev desert back to Bethel, in Canaan.

Abraham wondered how he could be the father of a great nation when he was an old man with no children at all.

But God kept His promise to Abraham and when Abraham was one hundred years old and Sarah was ninety, she bore him a son. They named him Isaac, which means "he laughs" because they knew people would laugh with them because they had a child in their old age.

Through the lineage of Isaac, Jesus was born. Jesus fulfilled God's promise to Abraham by being a "blessing to the whole world."

*We skipped the events that happened when they went into Egypt. Although these are important events in their lives, we skipped this part for simplicity's sake. The events in Egypt may need to be taught in their own lesson.

Applications

1. Abraham was willing to leave his comfort zone.

God was specific about whom and what Abraham would be leaving. He told him to leave his "country, people and family" (verse 12:1). In our culture today, we may not see the full significance of this command. Today, most of you reading this story have moved several times and to several different cities, but back then, the son would carry on his father's business and would never leave his home town. (Women would marry locally and stay put too...) They would hand down their land and possessions to keep it in the family. Only the very poor would roam abroad in search of a better life.

Scholars say Ur was a very developed city, with government, social activities, schools and pagan temples. It was located on the Euphrates River in modern day Iraq. God was calling Abraham to a new land where he had no claim to any land or social standing. This was intensified by the fact that he, like most people, was a livestock owner. Livestock need land to graze; Abraham did not know if he could find any to use when he arrived.

"Leave your country"

Ur had a good set of laws in place, but Abraham was being asked to leave their security. This was no small move to a nearby town God had in mind. God told Abraham to leave his country and start a new life in a new one. Interestingly enough, God didn't even tell Abraham where he was going, He just told him to go to "the land I will show you."

If God calls you to another country, will you go? Will you trust Him?

"Leave your people"

More than leaving the actual land upon which Abraham lived, he also had to leave his friends and acquaintances. I think one of the hardest things for a young person to do today is to leave the comfort zone of his friends - *his people*.

But God doesn't call us to look only inward at our own circle of friends, He wants us to reach out to those around us. We have a tendency to concentrate on our close friends and basically ignore everyone else. This is harmful in church groups and in the evangelism of the world. This phenomenon is especially strong in junior high and high school. Friendships mean everything to most young people. But God wants us to put Him first, even above our friends, and to follow Him instead of anyone else. Studies have shown that the thing most feared by teenagers is rejection by their peers. Because of that, many of them will do almost anything to fit in. This is why gangs are so prevalent and why most young people struggle so much with popularity and temptations.

Would you be willing to leave your friends during lunch and sit with a person who doesn't have many friends and is not popular? How would you feel if you were that person? (Some in your group undoubtedly know exactly what that feels like because they *are* that person.)

As the author has found out, popularity just changes its name after graduation. In adulthood, it is called "office politics" and the urge to fit in remains very strong.

"Leave your father's household"

This is no small sacrifice either. To move away from your extended family is not easy today and was much more difficult back then. But Jesus made it very clear that we are to put God above even our own families. He said, "Do you think I came to bring peace on earth? No, I tell you, but division. From now on there will be five in one family divided against each other, three against two and two against three. They will be divided, father against son and son against father, mother against daughter and daughter against mother, mother-in-law against daughter-in-law and daughter-in-law against mother-in-law" (**Luke 12: 51 - 53**).

Yes, we are to be peacemakers and yes, we are to honor our fathers and mothers, but we must ultimately put God first in all things. There is much conflict in many families today because some desire to follow God and others don't. Some have even been ostracized from their families because of their faith in Christ.

Abraham took his father with him (probably his mother too, although she may have died before he left), but had to leave most of his other relatives behind. He also took his wife (they didn't have any children). God would never call on a father or mother to abandon his or her children. That is not the case here at all.

Would you be willing to leave your family to follow God, if necessary?

2. God rewarded Abraham's faith by making him the father of many people.

God promised Abraham that his descendants would be more numerous than the stars in the sky. That's a pretty bold promise to a seventy-five-year-old man with no children at all! But we can see through history that God kept His promise: Abraham is the father of the Jews, the Arabs and the Christians. Abraham's offspring, Jesus, blessed the whole world, just like God said.

Abraham became a wealthy rancher with land, cattle, servants and friends. God gave him everything he gave up and much more. God also fulfilled His promise by giving Abraham a son whose offspring became the Jews and Christians. (Abraham's eldest son, Ishmael, was not a child of the promise, but of Abraham's lack of faith, but even *he* became the father of the Arab peoples.)

3. Abraham had to wait for God to fulfill His promises.

Yes, Abraham was blessed for his faith, but he had to wait many years to receive it. (Twenty-five years for Isaac to be born.) God always keeps His word, but we may have to be patient to receive it. Abraham's faith was tested and he didn't always pass, but ultimately, God was faithful and did what He said He would do.

You will notice the first thing that happened when Abraham arrived in Bethel was a famine occurred throughout the area. Abraham must have wondered why God told him to go to a place where he would starve. But God provided for him by sending him to Egypt for a time. Abraham didn't behave as he should have on the trip to Egypt, but he came back much wealthier, and therefore, more prepared to settle his own land. *God used the famine to provide Abraham with what he needed! Just when we think God has let us down, He uses what seems bad for our own good!*

4. It was Abraham's faith, not his actions that made him righteous.

If you read Abraham's story, you quickly see that he was not perfect. Not by a long shot. But he had faith in God and that's what counts. Perhaps the most important verse in the Bible about Abraham is **Genesis 15:6**, "Abram believed the Lord, and He credited it to him as righteousness." He believed God would do what He said He would do and he believed God would keep His promises. Having faith is how we should be like Abraham. *We should believe God just like he did and we should act upon our faith in obedience like he did, too.*

Paul says it is our *faith* that makes us right with God, not our works (**Ephesians 2:8,9**), although it is God's grace that actually saves us and not our faith. Faith is the vehicle God uses to give us His grace. The writer of Hebrews says it is impossible to please God without faith (**Hebrews 11:6**) and that the "ancients" are commended for having faith (**Hebrews 11:2**) - not for the works the faith produced. The works are only pleasing to God when they are done in faith. It was Abraham's faith, not his actions, that made him righteous in God's eyes.

 **Wrap-up.**

Abraham had faith and God was faithful. That sums up this story. We must believe God's promises and not take matters into our own hands. Instead, we must trust God in everything. Abraham was not perfect, but he had faith and that is what really counts.

Are you willing to leave the security of your friends and family to follow God? Are you willing to leave your comfort zones to obey Him? Will you wait patiently for God to fulfill His promises? If God says "go", will you go?

Optional Activity:

Before this session, have your students get up from where they are sitting and sit by someone they either don't know or don't normally sit by. Don't tell them why until after the lesson. Make sure your students all sit by someone new or different. (This same Optional Activity is found in *Yikes!*, session 19.)

A second option: (consider doing both.)

Have your students gather their Bibles, purses and books, take the chair they are sitting in (assuming you use metal folding chairs like the rest of us), go outside and walk around the church one time without talking. Tell them to meditate on *being obedient to God, even if it seems silly* as they walk.

When they come back in, have volunteers come to the front and talk about what God showed them during the assignment.

Make sure adult volunteers walk with them, for security purposes.

A third option:

If you teach this session during the school year, see if any students will volunteer to sit by someone at lunch one day this week who normally has to sit alone. Have the students who do so report back to the group during your next session.

Encourage your students to invite students who may not have friends into their lunch and friendship circles.

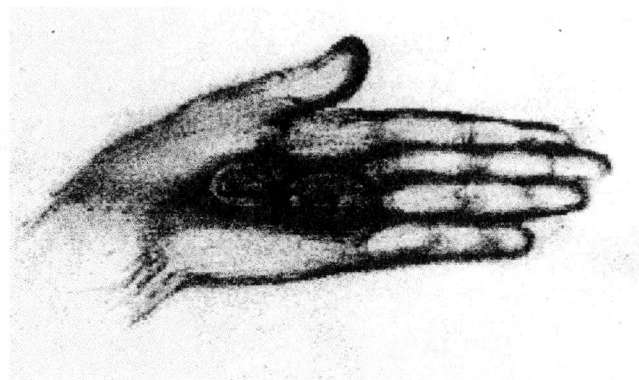

A Widow's Offering
Mark 12: 41 - 44

Jesus was sitting in the temple in Jerusalem watching as people came and put their offerings into the collection plate. Many rich men came and put in large amounts of money. A poor widow came and put in two small coins, worth less than a penny.

Jesus gathered His disciples to Himself and said, "I tell you the truth, this poor widow has put more into the treasury than all the others. You see, they gave out of their excess wealth, but she, in her poverty, gave all she had."

1. God doesn't need our money, He wants our hearts.

God can turn two small fish and five biscuits into a feast for thousands of people. He owns the cattle on a thousand hills. He is not poverty stricken or in need of our money to operate. He already owns it all. So what do you give to a person (or God) who already owns the whole world and everything in it? You give Him your heart. That's what He wants. That's what He demands. That's what this poor widow gave.

How do we know she gave God her heart - all the Bible says is that she gave two small coins (lepta, worth less than a penny)? The answer is implied in her action and Jesus' reaction. Yes, she gave a very small amount, but it was *all she had*. The wealthy who put in their money that day would probably never miss the money they gave; they had plenty more where that came from. But this poor woman gave all she had to live on. It was a *sacrifice* for her. She gave all she had to give (you can't give more than that) and it cost her. She may not have eaten that day because she gave her last penny to God. That's the type of giving that truly shows God our hearts: giving that costs us something.

2. If God already owns everything, why should we give Him anything?

God could miraculously drop money from the sky if He so chose. But He doesn't choose this. Instead, He lets our churches and ministries stand or fall based upon our giving. If the people of a church stop giving, the ministers' salaries cannot be paid, the light bill will not be paid, the secretaries will lose their jobs, the notes go bad and everyone must find a new place of worship. You see, if this happens, it must mean the people don't truly love God. We *will* give our time and money to what is important to us. You and I know this is true and so does God. He knows that if we truly love Him, we won't mind giving Him our time and money.

Let's take this a step further: If you truly love someone, you will give *sacrificially* to him. I never think of what I could be doing with all of the money I spend on my family. I gladly give them all I can because they are important to me and I love them.

God knows that if I really love Him, I won't mind giving Him all I can. I preached a sermon one time called "I Love you with all my Checkbook". The whole point was that we will give our money to what interests us and to what we care about. If we are interested in a certain hobby, we gladly give our money to support it. If we believe in a certain cause, we will support it financially. If we love a certain person, we will gladly give him money until it hurts. *If we love God, we will want to support His ministry on earth by our means.*

3. But wait, she only gave a small amount!

Again, it is not the size of the coin that matters, but the size of the sacrifice. God can take five loaves and two fish and turn it into a feast, and He can take two lepta and pay a youth minister for a year. (I know what you are thinking - that sounds like my salary, too! But hey, I haven't missed a meal yet and God does take care of us - multiplying the small amount the church folks pay us...)

God obviously doesn't commend or reward us for the amount of money we can give Him, instead He applauds us for the amount of sacrifice - because the amount of sacrifice shows our true devotion. That is all that matters to Him, since, as we said, He already owns it all anyway.

The Old Testament amount for a tithe was ten percent. In the New Testament, Paul said, "On the first day of every week, each one of you should set aside a sum of money in keeping with his income" (**I Corinthians 16:2**), and "Whoever sows sparingly will also reap sparingly, and whoever sows generously will also reap generously. Each man should give what he has decided in his heart to give, not reluctantly or under compulsion, for God loves a cheerful giver" (**2 Corinthians 9: 6,7**).

Paul decided in *his* heart to give everything he had to God; his wealth, possessions and life. God deserves more than just ten percent - He deserves it all. He wants us to give until it hurts and He wants us to enjoy giving to Him because that's how much we love Him. Then He will open the windows of Heaven and bless us (**Malachi 3:10**).

Wrap-up.

God doesn't need us to give, He already owns everything, but He *wants* us to give sacrificially to Him because that proves to Him and us our commitment to Him. God can take a small amount, given in love, and turn it into a tremendous blessing to others.

David, a man after God's own heart, said he would not give an offering to God that cost him nothing (**1 Chronicles 21:24**). The wealthy were giving more money to God in our story, but it didn't cost them what the small coins cost the widow and that was what impressed Jesus.

Optional Activity:

Pass out pens or pencils and sheets of paper. Have **all** of your students list three people in their lives who made sacrifices for them.

Instruct **half** of your students to write a brief essay on what life would be like if no one ever sacrificed for anyone else.

If you like, have a team write and perform a drama based on this idea.

Have the **other half** write an essay on ways they can sacrifice for God.

Give your students about ten minutes to write their essays and prepare the drama, then ask for volunteers to read their lists and essays.

You may need to help them think of people who have sacrificed for them by reminding them of their parents, grand-parents, soldiers who have fought and died for their freedom, the early Christians who suffered and died for the church and the Bible, pastors, teachers, brothers and sisters, friends, youth ministers, etc.

18

Joshua's Farewell Speech
Joshua 23 & 24

Joshua was old and well advanced in years. He had led the Israelite people into the promised land and was now enjoying peace. Israel had conquered all of its enemies, just as God had promised.

Now he knew it would soon be his time to die. He summoned all of the people of the nation to himself, including the elders, judges and officials. He reminded them what God had done for them.

"The Lord your God fights for you, just as He promised, so be careful to love Him with all of your hearts. Hold fast to Him, just as you have done until now," he told them.

"Be strong in the Lord," he told them, "and do not forget to follow all of His laws. Do not associate with the pagan nations near you or call on their gods. Do not intermarry with them or become political allies with them. If you do, the Lord will no longer fight for you."

Joshua reminded them of their history and how God and given them this land.

"Now, fear the Lord and serve Him with all faithfulness," Joshua told them. "Throw away the gods your forefathers worshiped beyond the river and in Egypt, and serve the Lord. But if serving the Lord seems undesirable to you, then choose for yourselves this day whom you will serve, whether the gods your forefathers served beyond the river, or the gods of the Amorites, in whose land you are living. But as for me and my house, we will serve the Lord."

The people cried out to Joshua that they would serve God and God alone.

Joshua took a large stone and set it under an oak tree near the holy place of the Lord.

"See!" he said to them, "this stone will be a witness against us. We have vowed to follow God in its presence. It will be a witness against you if you are untrue to your God."

# Applications

1. Hold on tight to the Lord your God.

Verse eight of chapter twenty-three sums up Joshua's life and message. It may have been easy to hold on tight to God when He was saving them from enemies and helping them advance on a new and exciting journey. Verse 24:12 says He sent hornets ahead of the army to drive the enemy away. God gave Jericho to them when they marched around it with trumpets. By God's power the walls fell. But Joshua knew they might forget about God in this time of peace.

Do you think of God only when you are in trouble - or do you hold tight to Him in good and bad times?

2. Be careful to love the Lord your God.

Often, when we think of God in Old Testament days, we think of Him bringing wrath and judgment on His people and enemies; an angry God flooding the earth and raining fire and brimstone on wicked cities. It's true that God is a God of judgment, but God loves us and wants us to love Him. *God wants a relationship with us and created us for that very purpose.*

Deuteronomy 6:5 says to love God "with all of your heart, soul and strength," **Hosea 6:6** says God wants our love more than our offerings, **Micah 6:8** says what God really wants from us is to walk with Him.

Joshua knew the most important thing a person can do is love God.

Do you love God and walk with Him, or do you only use Him in times of trouble?

3. God always keeps His promises.

God always keeps His promises to us. Is that good or bad news to you? Joshua pointed out that God kept His promises to sustain His people and give them the land He had promised, but He would also keep His promise to punish them if they forgot about him.

God's Word is full of promises to us. He promises to give us an eternal full life if we believe and trust in Him, but He also promises to bring judgment on those who forsake and ignore Him.

4. Choose this day whom you will serve.

The fact that God wants us to choose Him is proof that He loves us. He could *make* us love Him, but that wouldn't be real love. He wants us to choose Him because we *want* too. That is love. That's what God wants.

Joshua told the people to make a choice: Serve God or serve some other god. He told them they could serve the gods (really, idols) some of their parents had worshiped in Egypt or the gods of the people (the Amorites) who lived there before them. Or, they could choose to love and serve God and God alone. The point was: Make a choice. Pick one and give him your full devotion. Jesus told the church at Laodicea the same basic thing in **Revelation 3:16**. Jesus said we cannot serve both Him and money in **Matthew 6:24**.

Joshua said, "if serving the Lord seems undesirable to you, then choose for yourselves *this day* whom you will serve." (vs. 24:15) Joshua told the people to choose whom they wanted to serve and do it right then. God's call for allegiance is always today's call. Choose today whose side you are on. If you don't want to serve God, be prepared to face His promise for judgment, but if you choose to serve God, all of His promises for a full and eternal life await you.

Joshua knew the temptation would be strong to serve the gods their parents served. That same temptation is strong today. *Sometimes, young people have to reject their parents' gods (maybe money, material possessions, power, or false religions) to choose to follow God.*

Joshua also knew the temptation would be strong to serve the gods of the land in which they were living. *Who or what is the god of your country? Why is it such a strong temptation to follow after the world and not God?*

5. This stone will be a witness against you.

It is good to have a marker to help us remember a vow. A wedding ring should be a constant reminder of our marriage vows. In the Old Testament, the people would take a large stone and set it somewhere. Then, whenever they saw it, it would remind them of the promise they had made with God there that day.

We need markers in our lives to remind us of our vows. This may be a signature on a contract or a trip to the altar during church. It is also important that we hold each other accountable to our commitments. We should take our vows to God seriously and write it "in stone" that we will forever be faithful to Him.

 **Wrap-up.**

Joshua was about to die and wanted to make a final speech to the people of Israel whom he had been leading since Moses died. In his farewell address, he reminded the people of what God had done for them. He told them that God would keep His promises - good or bad - and instructed them to choose that very day whom they would serve. He told them that he and his family would always serve God no matter what the cost. He knew they would be tempted to forget God when things were going well and bow to gods of materialism and pleasure, so he set a stone under a tree as a reminder of their vow to serve, love and follow God.

Following God has never been easy, but we can do it in His strength.

Optional Activity:

In advance, find a large smooth stone. (Large enough for all of your students to sign.) If you live in an area where there aren't any to be found, you might buy a cinder block from a hardware store. Get a pen that will write on your rock or brick. A "tulip" craft pen will do the job.

Write the date of this session on the rock.

After the lesson, invite students to come to the front and say, **"as for me and my house, we will serve the Lord."**

After they have said this to the group, they will take the pen and sign their names to the rock. Set the rock in a corner of the room as a reminder of their vow to serve God. Remind them of the importance of keeping their vows to God.

A **second option** might be this: See if any student would like to write his own "farewell" speech. He or she can read this to the group during the next session. This speech would be a summation of what he thinks is most important in life.

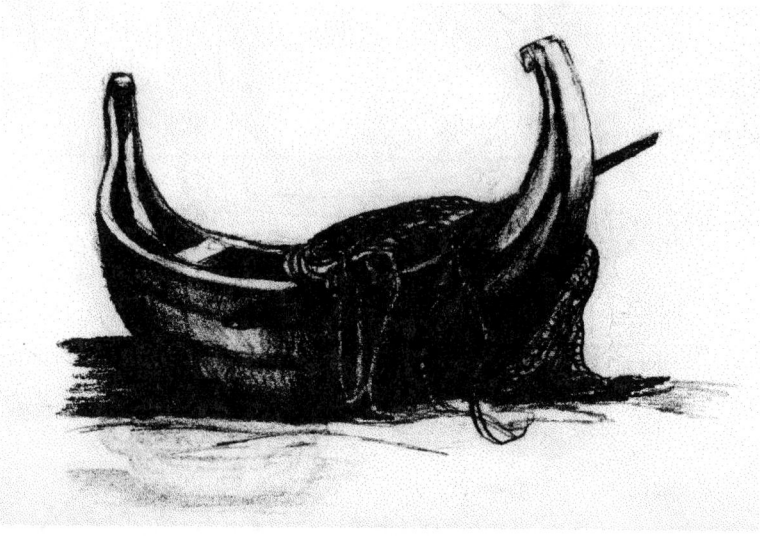

Jesus Calms a Storm

Mark 4: 35 - 41

One day Jesus was busy teaching and ministering to people. When evening came, He said to His disciples, "let's go over to the other side of the sea of Galilee." So, they got into a boat and started across. Other boats sailed with them, too. As they sailed across the lake, Jesus fell asleep on a cushion in the back of the boat.

Suddenly, a storm came upon them. The rain was so fierce and the waves were so large that the disciples feared the water would swamp and sink the boat.

So, they went and woke Jesus. "Master, don't you care that we are about to drown?" they cried out to Him.

Jesus got up and rebuked the storm, "Peace. Be still."

The storm immediately subsided and all was calm.

"Where is your faith?" He asked them, "why were you afraid?"

The disciples were both terrified and amazed at what Jesus had done.

"Who is this man," they asked each other, "that even the winds and the waves obey Him?"

1. Jesus is not worried about the things that worry us.

This is the only time in the Bible where we find Jesus taking a nap. He had been busy healing and preaching to people all day. It was late afternoon, probably hot, and Jesus was undoubtedly physically tired. We know that Jesus often prayed late into the night and got up early for more prayer time.

So, He took full advantage of this *down time* and stretched-out on a cushion in the back of the boat. When the storm struck, the coolness of the wind, rain and cloud-cover probably felt good to Him. There may have been a canopy at the back of the boat that was sheltering Jesus from the raindrops. Never the less, the fact that the storm didn't wake Jesus shows how deeply He was sleeping and how much at peace with the world He was. It was terrifying to the disciples, *but it didn't scare Jesus.* I heard a preacher say that God was simply rocking His baby boy with this storm! Yes, God (and therefore Jesus) deliberately created this storm and every other storm in history. That's why Jesus wasn't afraid.

We may think life is out of control when a "storm" comes our way. This story clearly shows that God is in control of everything, even events that we consider random, like storms. Nothing is random with God. He is in control of the cosmos, of nature, and of every other aspect of life in the universe. Jesus created the wind, the lightning, the water, the atmosphere, the wood the boat was made of, and the disciples who were in it. It is all His, created by Him and for Him (**Colossians 1:16**). He is not worried about the things we are.

2. Yes, Jesus cares if you are afraid.

It didn't take the disciples long to wake Jesus and ask Him if He cared that they were all about to drown. Jesus asked them why they were afraid. "Where is your faith?" He asked them after He calmed things down. From the narrative it doesn't seem like they expected Him to actually stop the storm, they just wanted Him to know that they were all about to die. They seemed to be saying, "how can you sleep when calamity is upon us?"

His response amazed and surprised them. "Who is this man, that even the wind and waves obey Him?" they asked. The only answer to that question is: God Himself.

The storm would have eventually awakened Jesus, but the disciples were wise to call upon Him to do something. *Even if you don't have any idea what Jesus can do for you, it is still wise to call on Him when you are in trouble.*

Jesus just may stop the storm that is upon you. *Sometimes Jesus calms the storm and sometimes He calms his child.* He may be using this particular storm to make you stronger and He may, therefore, choose not to stop it. But He might just stop the storm if you ask Him to. Go ahead, ask Him. He is right there in your boat. He may be at total peace with your world, but He will respond if you let Him know a storm is on you.

He cared that the disciples were afraid, and He cares if you are afraid. He is God and He can do what He pleases (**Psalm 115:3**), so let Him know when you are afraid.

3. Jesus creates worlds and stops storms with His spoken word.

One of the important lessons of this story is the power of Jesus' spoken word. All He had to do was say "peace, be still" and the storm and waves obeyed His wishes. This gives us a clue to His power. He *spoke* the universe into existence "ex nihilo" - out of nothing! (God used His hands to make people out of clay, so we are the only creatures that have His fingerprints on us!)

Don't be deceived, the most powerful force in the universe is the spoken word of God. Yet, God loves us and wants what is best for us. This should give us great comfort when we face life's storms. Nothing is a surprise to God and nothing catches Him off guard. He is the great I Am and He is willing and able to comfort us or even calm our storms if we will but cry out to Him.

I would rather be in the worst storm of the century with Jesus in my boat, than on the calmest of waters without Him.

 **Wrap-up.**

Jesus created everything in the universe for His own pleasure. The storm on the lake that day was bad enough to scare seasoned fishermen, but it didn't frighten Jesus. He started the storm and He stopped it. He has all the power of the universe and nothing is random to Him.

He cares when we are afraid and will comfort us. Sometimes He may choose to stop the storm and sometimes He may simply give us the strength to weather it, but He is always there for us if we will just cry out to Him.

Optional Activity:

Place a table or chair by the door with slips of blank paper and pens or pencils on it. As you students enter the room, have them take a slip of paper and pen or pencil and write on it a **storm** they are facing in their lives right now.

Tell them it can be a small squall line or a major hurricane. Tell them to keep their slips private for the time being.

After the lesson, ask your students to look at their slips of paper. Instruct them to write on the back a way God can calm their storms.

Pray with them about their storms and encourage them to have faith that God can solve any problem they may be facing.

If time permits and they wish to, they can discuss their storms with the group.

Jesus Heals Ten Lepers

Luke 17: 11 - 19

Jesus was on His way to Jerusalem, traveling along the border between Galilee and Samaria. As He was approaching a village, ten lepers stood at a distance and cried out to Him, "Jesus, Master, have pity on us!"

When He saw them, he said, "Go show yourselves to the priests."

As they were going, they were healed. One of them, when he saw that he was cleansed of the disease, came back, praising God as loud as he could. He threw himself at Jesus' feet and thanked him. And this man was a Samaritan.

Jesus asked him, "Were not all ten healed? Where are the other nine? You mean the only one to come back and give praise to God was this foreigner?

"Go," He said to the man, "your faith has made you well."

Applications

1. The men acted on their healing before it happened!

When we read this story, we are mostly disappointed with the way nine of the ten lepers acted. After all, they seemed ungrateful. But notice that they all ran toward town to see the Jewish priests *before* they were actually healed! This is a demonstration of the kind of faith God wants us to have. *To believe He is going to do what He says even before we see it happen.* This is exactly what **Hebrews 11:1** says faith is: "being sure of what we hope for and certain of what we do not see." The men may have been ungrateful, but they did have faith in Jesus. They showed that by crying out to Him in the first place and then by heading toward town to be declared clean before they even were.

You will recall that lepers could not get close to another person. They had to live in leper colonies and cry out "unclean!" if someone approached them. **Leviticus 14** tells how Jews who were cleansed of the disease must show themselves to the priest so that he could declare them healed. Today, we call leprosy *Hansen's disease*. It is caused by a bacteria and is very rare in western civilization. It is treatable with proper medicine, but back then there was no treatment, and they were understandably terrified of it.

2. Only one man came back.

It seems typical that only one of the nine came back to thank Jesus. So many Christians have so much to be thankful for, but few bother to stop and give God the praise that is due Him. God has given us eternal life; how can we ever show Him our gratitude for that? By giving Him our thanks before we do anything else. In other words, giving Him first place in our lives, the first fruits of our labor and the first part of our time. That's what the *one* did. The other nine just kept running.

Do you just keep running and enjoying your new life in Christ, or do you stop to thank and praise Him?

3. It was a Gentile foreigner who came back.

Let's face it, churches are full of people who are a bit spoiled. Perhaps they grew up in Christian families and have known little other than goodness, plenty and grace. *Sometime, it is the teenagers who grew up in church who are the most rebellious.* That's the way the Jews had become. They knew that God was their God and had become pious about it. They believed that God hated the Gentiles and loved only them. This story is yet another proof that God loves everyone equally. Jesus didn't ask to see their social security cards before He healed them, He just said "go!" to all of them.

The Jews were religious, but lacked the relationship with God that He desired.

As we know, the Jews rejected Jesus and do not accept Him as the Messiah (except for Messianic Jews). It is the Gentiles who have embraced Christ and accept Him for who He claimed to be. This story is symbolic of that fact.

The Jews hated and looked-down upon the Samaritans. Jesus told the story of the "good Samaritan" because of this.

This story is an example of those who are not religious embracing Christ and being thankful for what He has done for them. It is symbolic of all of us Gentiles who have embraced Christ and have been grafted onto the tree of God's family.

Are you just religious, or are you thankful to merciful God for His grace?

 **Wrap-up.**

When we read this story, we must ask ourselves if we are like the nine who kept going, or the one who came back to give God the praise for the new life He had just given.

Being a religious person will never be enough; that religion must accompany a relationship with God.

God's grace is abundant and free to all who will ask for it and accept it.

It is interesting to note that the social classes broke down in this story and the Samaritan was apparently hanging out with nine Jews. The Jews were outcasts themselves and realized at that point that all men truly were equal. When we realize that we are all sinners, we too should see each other as equals.

Optional Activity:

One of the main objects of this story is for us to see that we have a lot to be thankful for and we need to take time out to praise God for His blessings.

Hand out paper and pens or pencils. Have your students write down as many blessings as they can think of in ten minutes.

After the ten minutes are up, have the students read from their lists.

Challenge your students to find ways to show God their gratitude for His blessings.

Have your students list and discuss specific ways they can show God their gratitude for giving them new and eternal life.

Encourage your students to take their lists home and discuss this lesson with their parents.

21

Elijah and the Baal Prophets

1 Kings 18: 16 - 40

Elijah was the only prophet of the Lord God in Israel, but there were four hundred and fifty prophets of the god Baal and four hundred prophets of the god Asherah. King Ahab and his wife, Jezebel supported the Baal and Asherah prophets, but Jezebel hated Elijah.

The people of Israel were torn between the true God and the more popular god, Baal.

Elijah rebuked King Ahab, stating that he was ruining the country by refusing to worship the true God of Israel.

"Assemble all of the people of Israel and the eight hundred and fifty prophets of the Baals, who eat at Jezebel's table, at Mount Carmel," Elijah told the king.

King Ahab did as Elijah told him and assembled the prophets and people at the mountain.

Elijah cried out to the people that they needed to decide who they wanted to worship. "How long will you waver between two opinions?" he asked them. "If the Lord is God, then follow Him; but if Baal is god, follow him."

The people said nothing.

So Elijah told them, "Let the four hundred and fifty prophets of Baal place a bull on their altar. I will place a bull on the altar of God. Which ever god sends fire to consume his sacrifice, He is the true God."

The people declared that this was a good idea.

Elijah told the Baal prophets, "You go first. Take a bull and prepare it for sacrifice. Cut it to pieces and place it on the wood of your altar, but do not light the fire. Call on the name of your god and see if he will answer you."

The prophets began in the morning and cried out to their god all day long. At noon, Elijah began to taunt and make fun of them. "Perhaps your god is taking a nap, is deep in thought or traveling. Shout louder!"

The prophets shouted all the louder, dancing around the altar and even cutting themselves with swords and spears until they bled.

Nothing. No response.

In the evening, Elijah had had enough. He got the people's attention and repaired the altar of God which was there in ruins on the mountain. He placed twelve large stones on the altar, saying that the stones represented the twelve tribes of Israel that God had ordained.

Then he arranged the wood, cut the bull to pieces, and instructed people to dig a large trench around the altar. He had them pour water onto the sacrifice and wood. The water soaked the sacrifice and wood and filled the trench until it overflowed.

That evening when the time for sacrifice came, he prayed to God, "O Lord, God of Abraham, Isaac and Israel, let it be known today that you are God in Israel and that I am your servant and have done all things at your command. Answer me, O Lord, answer me, so these people will know that you, O Lord, are God and that you are turning their hearts back again."

Suddenly the fire of the Lord fell and burned up the sacrifice, the wood, the stones and the soil, and evaporated the water that was in the trench.

When the people saw this, they fell prostrate and cried, "The Lord - He is God! The Lord - He is God!"

So Elijah commanded the people, "Seize the prophets of Baal. Don't let any of them get away!"

The people grabbed the Baal prophets and took them to the Kishon Valley and slaughtered all of them there that day.

Applications

1. The majority of people are not always right.

The Baal prophets were more popular. Their gods didn't make the harsh demands that God did. There were more of them; they were government funded and they told the people what they wanted to hear. But they were wrong. They were following false gods and it cost them their lives.

The Baal gods symbolized power and fertility. The people found it easier to worship them because of this. They couldn't decide who to worship; seemed to be riding the fence. Elijah assembled them together and said "make a choice." We are commanded to make that very choice to this very day.

Even though God has all the power, people reject Him because of the claims He makes on their lives. The majority will never follow God. Jesus said so in **Matthew 7:13 - 14.** Young people today have to make this same choice: *Choose to worship the true God or the gods of the majority.* It may cost them popularity at school and on the job. It may cause serious conflicts in their homes (**Matthew 10:21 - 22**). It costs some people their lives. It will never be easy to follow God, but it will always be right.

2. One man with God *is* the majority.

Elijah stood alone that day on Mount Carmel. Him against eight hundred and fifty false prophets, plus all of the people of Israel. But he won the day. Not because *he* had any power to do so, but because he stood up for the true God. It is true that we will probably lose some popularity when we are on God's side, but we will certainly win the ultimate victory.

The Bible is full of stories like this one where one person takes his stand for God against the powers of the enemy. These struggles are never easy and take true courage and faith, but with God, the victory is won.

Do you have the courage to take a stand for God, even if none of your friends stand with you?

3. God demonstrates His power to bring His children home to Him.

Elijah's prayer gives us a clue as to why God went along with this contest and showed His power that day. He did so to bring His people back to Himself. As we have seen from other stories, this is what God wants from us - a relationship. You may say, "But I've never seen God send fire from the sky!" Maybe not, but you have His Word and that is every bit as big a miracle as this particular event. Many of us *have* seen God perform other incredible miracles, but, again, God uses them to strengthen our faith and draw us closer to Him. The *resurrection*, though, is the only sign we need and the only sign Jesus promised us (**Matthew 12:39 - 40**). The overwhelming evidence of the resurrection is all we need to have faith like Elijah.

 **Wrap-up.**

You may feel at times that you are the only person on God's side. But this story reminds us that God has all of the power and it doesn't matter what most people think. God's prophets may never be politically correct or government-funded, but they will always be on the right side.

Elijah called on the people to choose between the true God and the gods of the land.

God demonstrated His power to remind the people that He is the true God and that He wants to have a personal relationship with us.

Being wrong cost the Baal prophets their lives. When people choose not to serve Holy God, they will always pay with their lives (**Romans 6:23**).

Optional Activity:

Write this statement on a black board, white board or poster board:

GOD IS INTOLERANT
JOHN 14:6

Explain to your students what *tolerance* is and how politically correct it is in today's world.

> Tolerance is the thought that what is right for me may not be right for you. It is the idea that everyone's lifestyle is okay if it doesn't hurt another person. It is the idea that truth for me may not be truth for you, depending on your situation. Intolerance is very politically incorrect today. People will say you are narrow-minded or even a bigot if you are intolerant.

Divide your students into teams. Give them paper and pens or pencils. Instruct them to select leaders for each team. Send them to different rooms or areas and have each team write an essay or drama on the statement on the board. Tell them to look up John 14:6 as a reference.

Give them ten to fifteen minutes to complete their tasks. When the ten minutes are up, have everyone come back together and present their essays or dramas. Encourage each person to participate in some way.

Teaching Tips:

If you are familiar with the rest of this story, you know that Jezebel was furious at Elijah for killing her prophets, so she threatened his life. You would think that after this powerful event, he would have told her to come and give it her best shot! Instead, he ran scared into the desert.

This is typical of Bible stories and of life today: After we have seen God win some mighty victory in our lives, we will usually face an attack from Satan. He hates it when God wins battles and doesn't take losses lightly. After students come home from camp or a spiritual retreat, they can expect some warfare. Elijah stood against eight hundred and fifty prophets in front of all of the people of his country, but he ran scared at the threat of one woman.

It seems that we usually have a trial to face after a mountaintop experience. Jesus was tempted right after being baptized and then fasting for forty days. Noah got drunk shortly after leaving the ark. Jonah threw a temper tantrum right after surviving being fish-food. The people of Israel abandoned God's principals just days after they walked across the dry bottom of the Red Sea.

Why is it, like Elijah, we soon forget the mighty things we see God do?

Be careful when talking about God's intolerance. God hates sin, but loves sinners. The object of this activity is to help your students see that the only way to heaven is through Jesus; it is not to put down, belittle or laugh at someone because his beliefs are different than yours.

We should be tolerant of one another in the sense that we forgive and love each other no matter what, but we can't believe God's word and also believe that everyone will reach heaven if they just try. Truth does not change - it is truth for everyone, no matter the circumstances. God says what truth is because He *is* truth. That's what makes Him intolerant.

The Woman at the Well

John 4: 1 - 42

Jesus had been in Jerusalem for the Passover celebration; now, He headed north toward his home base, Galilee. Most Jews went around Samaria, hating the people there, but Jesus walked right through the heart of the country.

At noon one day, He and His disciples came to a town called Sychar (pronounced sigh' car), and Jesus sat down by a well there that had belonged to Jacob. Jesus sent His disciples into town to buy some food.

Suddenly a Samaritan woman appeared. She had come to the well to get water.

"Will you give me a drink?" Jesus asked her.

"You are a Jew and I am a Samaritan," she said, "how can you ask me for a drink?"

She knew that Jews did not associate with Samaritans.

"If you knew who I was and the gift of God I possess, you would ask me and I would give you living water," Jesus replied.

"But you don't even have a bucket," she protested, "and this well is deep. Where can you get this living water? Are you greater than our father Jacob, who fed his flocks and herds here?"

Jesus answered, "Anyone who drinks of this water will be thirsty again, but whoever drinks of the water I give will never thirst again. In fact, the water I give him will become a spring of water within him, welling up to eternal life."

The woman said, "Sir, give me this water so I won't get thirsty and have to keep coming here to draw water."

"Go call your husband and then come back," Jesus said to her.

"But I have no husband," she said.

"You are right to say that," Jesus answered, "for you have had five husbands and the man you are now living with is not your husband."

"Sir," she changed the subject, "You must be a prophet since you know so much about me. Our fathers worshiped on this mountain, but you Jews claim that the place where we must worship is in Jerusalem."

"Believe me," Jesus replied, "a time is coming very soon when you will worship the Father neither on this mountain nor in Jerusalem. Salvation has come from the Jews and the time has now come when true worshipers will worship God in spirit and truth - they are the kind of worshipers for whom God is looking. God is Spirit and His worshipers must worship Him in spirit and in truth."

"I know the Messiah is coming," she said, "and when He does, He will explain everything to us."

"I am the Messiah," Jesus answered her.

About that time the disciples returned. They were surprised to see Jesus talking to a woman, but were afraid to question Him about it.

The Samaritan woman left her jar at the well and ran into town, proclaiming to all she saw, "Come, see a man who told me everything I ever did. Could He be the Messiah?"

So the people of town came out to see Jesus.

Meanwhile, the disciples asked Jesus if He wanted to eat.

"I have food that you know nothing about," He told them.

They didn't understand what He meant.

"My food is to do the will of the Father who sent me and to do His work. Open your eyes and see that the fields are ripe unto harvest. Others have already sown God's work and now I am sending you to reap the harvest. The sower and the reaper will rejoice together when God harvests a crop of eternal lives."

Meanwhile, because of the woman's testimony, many came to see Jesus. They urged Him to stay and He did. He and His disciples stayed with them for two days. Many people in that town heard Him and became believers.

They told the woman they believed in Jesus because they heard Him themselves and not just because of her testimony.

Applications

1. Jesus doesn't care about politics, He cares about people.

It was politically incorrect for Jesus to talk to this woman for two reasons: First, Jews did not like or talk to Samaritans; second, men did not talk to women in public. Jesus could have seriously damaged His reputation by talking to this woman, but He cared more about her soul than His reputation. She obviously had a bad name because she was coming for water in the heat of the day. Back then, women went for water early in the morning and late in the evening when it was cool. They traveled in groups like girls do to this day, but she was alone.

Would you threaten your position at school to reach someone who is not liked?

It is good to note here, though, that Jesus' behavior was appropriate and out in the open during the day. It was not as though Jesus met with her in secret. Students must be careful when reaching out to "sinners" that they do not fall into temptation. To speak to her was politically incorrect, but it was *morally* very correct.

2. Jesus gives us living water.

The Samaritan woman didn't understand what Jesus meant by living water. He was using an analogy of the water from the well and "water" that would forever quench her thirst. What did He mean? Jesus' living water was a reference to being eternally satisfied. When you drink of Jesus' water, you never have to wonder what the purpose for life is again. Your search for truth is over. Jesus' water satisfies our longing for truth and meaning, and gives us a joy and satisfaction we have never known before. The living water flows from within - which means it is not dependent on our circumstances - and it leads to eternal life. It is a beautiful picture of a Savior giving us eternal joy in a world that is continually thirsting but not being satisfied.

3. God is seeking true worshipers.

There are a couple of things very significant in this part of the story. Jesus said we didn't have to worship God any longer in a particular location. When Jesus was on the cross, the veil in the temple was torn in two. Now, we have access to God wherever we are. We can worship God in the privacy of our own homes or in a huge church. God looks at our hearts and that is all that matters.

(I am not saying it is not important to go to church to worship. **Hebrews 10:25** says we should meet together for worship. I'm just saying we don't have to go to Jerusalem or another particular place to truly worship Him.)

The other important doctrine Jesus teaches here is that God is seeking worshipers. This is a major concept and should not be overlooked. Usually, we think of *us* seeking God - many churches are now seeker sensitive - but here, Jesus says *God* is doing the seeking, and He is seeking those who worship Him in spirit and in truth.

So, what does *that* mean? Jesus answered, in part, for us: God is Spirit, so we must worship Him in *spirit*. If we worship God with our spirits, this refers to our attitudes more than our actions.

It could also mean that we must please the Holy Spirit in our worship - we must worship God and God alone. Our total focus and devotion must be on pleasing God every day; something we need the Holy Spirit's help in doing.

Worshiping Him in *truth* means we are emulating God in our actions (because God is truth) and are embracing good doctrine. A person may be totally sincere in his worship of Allah, but God does not accept that worship because it is not in truth. Jesus said only He can take us to the Father. No other religion provides true worship. God is looking for people who worship Him with all of their hearts, souls and minds and who have accepted Jesus as their only Savior.

Worship, then, goes beyond a church service. It is something we choose to do every minute of every day. *God is looking for worshipers and I want Him to see me and be pleased.*

4. A woman with a bad reputation led most of the town to Christ.

Did you catch that in this story? Women weren't even allowed to speak to a man in public, but this woman, with a bad reputation, led "half the town" to Christ! As we have stated before, God can use anyone He pleases. All of the preachers in that town combined never led as many people to Christ as she did!

Why? Because she met Jesus face to face and He forever changed her life. All she told people was, "Come, see a man who told me everything I ever did. Could

He be the Christ?" That was all she had to say. She told them what Jesus said to her and that He claimed to be the Messiah. That's what a witness is: A person who tells you what he saw or heard.

Her reputation and gender didn't matter because it wasn't about her, it was all about Jesus. That's how we can win our towns for Christ, by telling people what Jesus has done for us and who He claims to be.

 **Wrap-up.**

Jesus is not prejudiced. He loves everyone equally. He cares more about people than even His own reputation.

He explained some very important doctrine to this ordinary woman: That God provides living water that quenches our thirst for truth and meaning; and that God is seeking worshipers who will worship Him in spirit and in truth.

It has been said that we all have a God-shaped hole in our hearts, and only God Himself can fill it and quench our longing for Him.

Despite her reputation, the woman proclaimed to her town that Jesus was the Messiah, and many people accepted Him because of her testimony. God can and does use anyone.

Optional Activity:
Make copies of the Bible puzzle on the following page and hand them out to your students. Challenge them to find as many books of the Bible within it as they can. If you wish, offer a prize for the ones who find the most.

Key: Here are the 25 books you will find, in order: Amos, Mark, Luke, John, Joel, Judges, Job, Hebrews, Esther, Acts, James, Ruth, Romans, Titus, Matthew, Genesis, Hosea, Lamentations, Revelation, Timothy, Samuel, Numbers, Malachi, Peter, Kings.

Can You Find 25 Books of the Bible?

Can you find the names of 25 books of the Bible in this paragraph? This is a most remarkable puzzle. Someone found it in the seat pocket on a flight from Los Angeles to Honolulu, keeping himself occupied for hours. One man from Illinois worked on this while fishing from his john boat. Roy Clark studied it while playing his banjo. Elaine Victs mentioned it in her column once. One woman judges the job to be so involving, she brews a cup of tea to help calm her nerves. There will be some names that are really easy to spot...that's a fact. Some people will soon find themselves in a jam, especially since the book names are not necessarily capitalized. The truth is, from answers we get, we are forced to admit it usually takes a minister or scholar to see some of them at the worst. Something in our genes is responsible for the difficulty we have. Those able to find all of them will hear great lamentations from those who have to be shown. One revelation may help, books like Timothy and Samuel may occur without their numbers. And punctuation or spaces in the middle are normal. A chipper attitude will help you compete. Remember, there are 25 books of the Bible lurking somewhere in this paragraph.

Jesus the Twelve-Year-Old

Luke 2:41 - 52

Every year, Joseph and Mary took Jesus and His brothers and sisters to Jerusalem to the Feast of Passover. When Jesus was twelve years old, they went as always. When the feast was over, they began their return home to Nazareth. But Jesus stayed behind, talking with the teachers there. The teachers were amazed at His answers and understanding. Jesus sat and listened to them and asked them questions.

When they had traveled for a day, Joseph and Mary realized that Jesus was not with them. They began looking for Him among their relatives and friends. Then they returned to Jerusalem to look for Him. On the third day they found Him in the temple courts, sitting among the teachers.

His parents were astonished. Mary asked Him, "Son, why have you treated us this way? Your father and I were scared to death, looking everywhere for you!"

"Why were you searching for me?" He replied, "Didn't you know I would be in my Father's house?"

His parents didn't understand all of this.

Then Jesus went home with them and was obedient to them. Mary treasured these things in her heart. Jesus, meanwhile, grew in wisdom and stature, and in favor with God and men.

Applications

1. Jesus listened to the teachers and asked them questions.

This is the only story we have about Jesus during his adolescence. John and Mark start with Jesus as a grown man; Matthew skips from age two to age 30. Only Luke gives us this glimpse of Him as a preteen, and what a punch this short story packs!

First, we read that Jesus *listened* to the teachers in the temple courts. (vs. 46) Do you have any students who simply won't listen to the lesson? If your students want to be like Jesus, they must start by listening to their Bible study teachers. But not only did He listen, He also asked them questions. This shows that He was interested in the topic and what they had to say about it. *Even preteens can be interested in God's word!* Jesus certainly was. Jesus was so engrossed in the Bible study, He missed the bus home.

> How could Joseph and Mary leave Jerusalem without Him?
>
> A 12-year-old was considered both a man and a child. The children traveled in the front of the caravan with the women and the men traveled behind them. Joseph assumed Jesus was with Mary and she assumed He was with the men. There would have been several families from Galilee in this caravan, since there was safety in numbers.
>
> Remember the scene in *Home Alone* when they finally realized that Kevin was not with them? It could happen easily enough.
>
> Did Jesus sin by causing His parents to worry?
>
> No, Jesus didn't cause them to worry, they did. *They* left Him. He didn't run away from them, He simply didn't leave the temple when they thought He did.
>
> Jesus' answer to His mother may sound "short" to us, but He was simply stating the fact that He had to take advantage of being in the temple to learn all He could. He wasn't running the streets looking for trouble, He was in church.

2. The teachers were amazed at His understanding.

It shouldn't surprise us that this God-child had incredible understanding and insight about the Father and His Word. But this is a goal for your students: To be like Jesus. Wouldn't it be great if your students were known for their understanding of the Bible? Jesus must have been attentive as a child when His parents and teachers taught Him the truths of the Old Testament. He knew the stories and He memorized the verses. We know this because Jesus often quoted scripture. This passage tells us that He began His learning as a child and didn't wait until He was grown to do so.

The earlier your students begin learning scripture, the better off they will be.

3. Jesus obeyed His parents.

This passage tells us in black and white that Jesus was obedient to His parents (vs. 51). *If a student wants to be like Christ, he must be obedient to his parents.* God told us to honor our father and mother in **Exodus 20:12**. Paul told us to obey our parents in **Ephesians 6:1** and **Colossians 3:20**.

Why is it so important to God that we obey our parents? First, our parents are older and wiser than we are, and obeying them protects us and may even preserve our lives. Second, obeying our parents teaches us to obey God.

Your students need to understand that they cannot love and obey God if they do not love and obey their parents.

Here, in this story, Jesus once again sets the example.

Notice though that Jesus chose God over His parents. If a student or child has to make this choice, he should choose what God wants over the wishes of his parents. This is not an issue that should be taken lightly, and children should almost always obey their parents, but if a parent asks a child to do something contrary to God's Word, the child is obligated to obey God.

Paul told us adults to obey the law of the land (**Romans 13:1**), but we should break it if it is contrary to God's law. Again, this issue should never be taken lightly and there will be consequences to face if we disobey our parents or the government because of our loyalty to God. (I don't mean God's judgment, I mean punishment from our parents or the government.)

Because of His obedience and godly spirit, Jesus was respected by everyone and was known for His wisdom and graceful attitude. This does not sound too much like the typical teenager, but it is our example.

Now we know what a Christ-like teenager and preteen should be like.

 **Wrap-up.**

This story clearly shows us what Jesus was like as a twelve-year-old. He was intensely interested in God's Word and work; He was obedient to His parents; He was respected by everyone for his grace and wisdom; He listened to His teachers; He asked them questions; He loved being in church; He had insight into God's Word.

This then is what teens and preteens should be like today.

Optional Activity:

Divide your students into teams of five to 10 students. Give them paper and pens or pencils and send them to different rooms or areas. Have each team elect a leader or spokesperson.

Tell them to write "**Home Alone In Jerusalem**" on the top of their papers. Instruct them to write a play, essay, song or poem about this story. They can make the story "modern day" or keep it first century.

Give them ten to fifteen minutes to complete the task, then bring them all back together and have them read, sing or perform their projects.

Teaching Tips:

Isn't it interesting that He was "lost" for three days and then found again? Where did He stay those two nights? Priests lived at the temple back then and Jesus must have stayed there with them. They apparently fed and sheltered Him.

It is also interesting to note that Mary called Joseph Jesus' father in verse 48, but Jesus answered that He was in His Father's house. Jesus knew all along that His real father was God Himself. Jesus didn't evolve into the Christ, He was born that way. Even as a child, He apparently understood that He was God in the flesh. Mary and Joseph didn't fully understand what His mission was, but knew there was something extraordinary about this child.

Joseph apparently died before Jesus turned 30 because he is not mentioned during Jesus' ministry. Notice that Jesus obeyed Joseph as a child and teenager, even though he wasn't His real father. This sets the precedent that children must obey their stepparents, too.

Notice, too, that Jesus had conflict with His parents in this story. He didn't try to hurt them, but it happened. It should encourage parents that even Jesus caused His parents grief when He was a preteen. Part of adolescence is the pain of the growing, but natural, separation of children and their parents. Without this conflict, children would never mature to independence.

24

The Holy Spirit Comes
Acts 1: 4 - 9, 2: 1 - 16, 41

On one occasion, after Jesus had been resurrected, He appeared to His disciples and told them to stay in Jerusalem until the Holy Spirit came upon them.

"John baptized with water, but in a few days, you will be baptized with the Holy Spirit," He told them.

The disciples still didn't understand that His Kingdom was a spiritual one and asked Him if He was about to establish Israel's rule.

"The hour for that is not for you to know," He told them, "but soon, the Holy Spirit will come and give you power. You will become my witnesses in Jerusalem, Judea, Samaria and to the ends of the earth."

After He told them this, He rose up into the clouds before their eyes.

On the day of Pentecost, the disciples were together in a house. Suddenly, the sound of great wind filled the house and what appeared to be tongues of fire fell from heaven upon them.

When the Holy Spirit came upon them, they began to speak in languages they could not normally speak. There were many God-fearing Jews in the city that day and they heard the noise and went to investigate. These Jews were from every known country and each one could hear the message of Christ in his own language.

"Aren't these men from Galilee?" they asked each other. "How is it they can speak in all of these languages? What does this mean?"

Some tried to explain it by saying the men were drunk.

Then Peter stood and addressed them. "How can these men be drunk?" he asked. "It is only nine in the morning. No, they are not drunk, but filled with the Holy Spirit!"

Then Peter started with Old Testament scriptures and explained to them the good news about Jesus and how He died for them to cover their sins - and how God had raised Him from the dead.

When the people heard this, they were cut to the heart and asked Peter and the disciples, "What shall we do?"

Peter explained to them that they must repent of their sins and be baptized in the name of Christ. Three thousand men accepted Christ and were baptized that day.

Applications

1. The Holy Spirit is a person.

This great Bible story gives you the opportunity to teach some good doctrine to your students. The Holy Spirit is not an "it". He is a He. He is part of the Holy Trinity. He is the living, unseen, Spirit of God. He comes to live within our own spirits at the point of salvation (vs. 38, and **John 14:17**). He guarantees that if we accept Christ, we will go to heaven when we die (**Ephesians 1:13, 14**).

He teaches us all things (**John 14:26**).
He reminds us of what Jesus taught us (**John 14:26**).
He convicts us of sin (**John 16:8**).
He guides us into all truth (**John 16:13**).
He will bring glory to God (**John 16:14**).

He also empowers us to witness, helps us worship, compels us to be saved, helps us pray, brings unity to believers, helps us discern false teaching and brings true and lasting peace to believers.

Jesus promised that the Holy Spirit would come and called Him the Counselor (**John 14:16, 26, 15:26, 16:7**). Jesus said the Holy Spirit would not come until He, Jesus, went back to the Father (**John 16:7**).

The Holy Spirit was present, of course, during all of history, but came in a special, permanent way, as Jesus had promised, on the day of Pentecost. Before Pentecost, the Holy Spirit would come only on special occasions. Believers in the Old Testament did not have Him living in their lives as we do today.

(Old Testament believers were saved by grace, through faith that the Christ *would* come. Today, we are saved by grace, through faith that the Christ *did* come. People who lived before Jesus' death and resurrection could go to heaven by God's grace if they believed in God's promised Christ. We have always been saved by God's *grace* and that alone, but our faith is the *vehicle* God uses to give us His free gift of salvation.)

2. The Holy Spirit turns cowards into lions of the Faith.

Just fifty days earlier, Peter denied he even knew Jesus. After the Holy Spirit came upon him, he stood and preached Christ boldly in front of all of these strangers. History tells us that, eventually, Peter gave up his life for Christ. This is proof that Jesus was resurrected and evidence of the presence of the Holy Spirit in his life.

It was not just Peter, though. All of the disciples had run scared the night Jesus was arrested. (Judas had already hanged himself.) All of them boldly preached Christ for the rest of their lives and all of them but John were martyred because of it. The Holy Spirit gives us a spirit of love, power and self-discipline and not timidity (**2 Timothy 1:7**). *If your students will allow the Holy Spirit to do so, He will give them the courage to win their friends and families to Christ.*

Peter was not a scholar, but a fisherman, yet he stood and preached and three thousand people were saved! The Holy Spirit enables us to present the gospel and draws sinners to Himself.

3. The Holy Spirit comes into our lives the moment we are saved.

The Holy Spirit came in a visible, mighty way on the day of Pentecost. This was His entry into the church of God. Ever since then, we receive the Holy Spirit into our lives (hearts) at the moment of salvation. In **Acts 10:46 - 48**, Peter said, "Can anyone keep these men from being baptized with water? They have received the Holy Spirit just as we have." The men had been saved, could speak in tongues and had received the Holy Spirit *before* they were baptized. This shows that baptism is an outward sign of what has happened on the inside and that salvation occurs *before* baptism and not because of it.

Some say there is a *second* filling of the Holy Spirit, after salvation. While it is true that we can *grieve* the Spirit (**Ephesians 4:30**), there is no scriptural evidence of a second filling. Being filled with the Spirit is something we must do daily as we give Him control of our lives (see the Teaching Tips after this chapter). We receive the Holy Spirit at the moment of salvation and He is part of our lives from then throughout eternity (**Ephesians 1:13, 14, 2 Corinthians 5:5, Ephesians 4:30**). But God is a gentleman and only takes control of the thoughts and actions that we give Him.

Romans 8:9 says we have the Spirit of Christ in our lives if and only if we belong to Christ. If we are saved, we have the Holy Spirit in our lives as a seal, promise, comforter, counselor, helper, guide and empowerer. The Holy Spirit makes us a new creation at the moment of salvation (**2 Corinthians 5:17**).

 **Wrap-up.**

The Holy Spirit came upon the church at Pentecost and has given power and courage to Christians ever since. Since the Holy Spirit is God, He has always existed, but He came in a special and unique way at Pentecost. Since that day, we receive the Holy Spirit at the moment of salvation. Jesus promised that the Comforter would come soon and told His disciples to stay in Jerusalem until He did.

With the Holy Spirit's help, we have the power to witness and to live the Christian life every day. He is the "batteries" we need to work - the power source we must plug into for strength, courage and guidance. We are ineffective in our Christian walk when we grieve the Holy Spirit by living our lives like *we* want and not as He would have us.

Optional Activity:

Make copies of the hand-out sheet *Witnessing Practice* (page 146) so that each of your students can have a copy.

Hand out the sheet to your students and pair them by twos. If you have an odd number of students, you may be a partner.

Have them sit across from each other and take turns using the sheet to practice witnessing to each other, one student being "student one" and the other, "student two", then switching places.

Tell them that this is practice so they will know what to do in a real witnessing situation, but remind them that the Holy Spirit will guide them in what to say.

Encourage them to take this practice seriously as eternity is at stake.

After the practice, see if any student has just accepted Christ as Savior and if so, follow through.

Witnessing Practice

<u>Please role play from this script, then switch places and do it again:</u>

    Student **One**:   A Christian student leading a friend to Christ.
    Student **Two**:   A lost person who is interested in becoming a Christian.

(Student **One**) If you died today, where do you think you would go?
    *(Student **Two**) I'm really not sure, but I think heaven.*
(Student **One**) Why?
    *(Student **Two**) Well, I've always been a pretty good person. I've never killed anyone or anything like that.*
(Student **One**) Here's what the Bible says: **Romans 3:23** says <u>all</u> have sinned and fallen short of God's glory.   **Romans 6:23** says the punishment for that sin is death, but **Romans 6:23** also says Jesus will pay for our sins if we will let Him. **Romans 5:8** says God loved us - even before we knew Him, and **Romans 10:13** says everyone who calls on the name of the Lord will be saved.
    *(Student **Two**) Do you think God would really send anyone to hell?*
(Student **One**) Yes, the Bible says we will go to hell if we don't believe in Jesus. Jesus said "I am the way and the truth and the life and no one comes to the Father except through me," in **John 14:6** . And He said "For God so loved the world that He gave His one and only Son, that whoever believes in Him will not perish but have eternal life" in **John 3:16**. God made us and loves us, but He will not let us into His heaven unless we accept Jesus as our savior. We cannot save ourselves. Only Jesus can save us. Do you believe in Jesus?
    *(Student **Two**) Yes, I do.*
(Student **One**) Do you believe Jesus will save you if you ask Him?
    *(Student **Two**) Yes, I do.*
(Student **One**) Do you believe you are a sinner and you cannot save yourself?
    *(Student **Two**) Yes, I do.*
(Student **One**) Then repeat this prayer after me and really mean it:

    Jesus -- I know I am a sinner -- I know I cannot save myself -- I believe that Jesus died for me -- and rose again. -- I ask you now -- to forgive me of my sins -- come into my heart -- and save me -- and I promise -- that from now on -- I will try -- to live for you -- thank you Jesus -- amen -- .

*(Student **Two** repeats each phrase.)*

Now see if you can go through this role play exercise by memory!

Teaching Tips:

This passage brings up a couple of questions. First, were the disciples "speaking in tongues" when the Holy Spirit came upon them? Some scholars believe they were speaking in actual languages they did not know. Others believe the Jews in the crowd *heard* the gospel clearly in their own languages although the disciples were "babbling" unknown words. (Most of the people in the crowd would have spoken Aramaic, the language of the Jews - and the language Peter and the disciples - but God made His message clear to all, no matter their language.)

Because some thought they were drunk (vs 13), many scholars believe they were speaking in an ecstatic, babbling, unknown language that God made clear in the *ears* of the hearers. Either way, this was a unique day in history that will not be repeated. Peter's sermon was clearly spoken and understood by all.

Second, does this story teach that every Christian will be able to speak in tongues? Paul makes it clear that he had the gift of speaking in unknown tongues, a sort of babbling that only the person and God can understand (**I Corinthians 14**), but he says not every Christian will have this gift (**1 Corinthians 12:28 - 31**). He also says there must be order in worship services and that someone must interpret if a person speaks in tongues in public (**1 Corinthians 14:27, 28**). Paul further says we should not forbid someone from speaking in tongues in a worship service (**1 Corinthians 14: 39**), so long as there is an interpretation and order.

To teach, though, that a person must be able to speak in tongues to prove he is a Christian is not teaching what Paul taught at all. Some Christians can speak in tongues and some cannot. **1 Corinthians 14** is clear on that issue. Everyone in the Corinthian church had been baptized, but not everyone could speak in tongues.

Third, why did the Holy Spirit come on the day of Pentecost? There is some rich symbolism here: Pentecost occurred on the Feast of Harvest which symbolized the giving to God of our *firstfruits*. The three thousand Jews who were saved that day were the firstfruits of a new harvest.

Also, the Feast of Harvest became associated with the day God gave Moses the Ten Commandments fifty days after Israel left Egypt (following Passover). The Bible doesn't say this happened fifty days later (Pentecost means, in Greek, *the fiftieth day*), but that association became accepted. The New Testament Pentecost was when God gave His Spirit to all believers, fifty days after Jesus' crucifixion and ten days after His ascension. (Remember though, the Holy Spirit has always been present, but He came in a *new* way at Pentecost.)

The law *tutored* us until the Spirit came and then we no longer were bound by it for righteousness (**Galatians 3:24 - 25; 4:1 - 7**).

Because Peter preached that day to an international crowd, three thousand people from around the world were saved and took the gospel home - giving Christianity an immediate, global boost.

Fourth, was this a second filling or the first filling for the disciples? Jesus had earlier breathed His Spirit into them (**John 20:21, 22**). Most scholars agree this was a temporary filling intended only for the disciples because of who they were and the faith they needed until Pentecost. The Spirit had always filled people's lives for special purposes, but He came in a new, permanent way at Pentecost.

Now, we are baptized (immersed) in the Spirit only once - at salvation - but we can be *filled* with the Spirit on a daily basis. To be *filled* with the Spirit is to be *controlled* by Him (**Ephesians 5:18**). Being baptized in Him means He comes to live inside of our spirits (**Ephesians 4:30, Romans 8:9, John 14:17**). Once He comes to dwell in us, He is there for all of eternity.

Jesus is Born

Luke 2: 1 - 20

In those days, Caesar Augustus issued a decree that a census be taken of everyone in the Roman world. Quirinius was governor of Syria at this time. So everyone had to go to his home town to register. The Romans would use this registration information for tax and military purposes.

Joseph, who lived in Nazareth in Galilee, went to Bethlehem in Judea because he was from the ancestry of David. He took his fiance', Mary, with him. She was far along in her pregnancy (this by the Holy Spirit - Joseph did not have sexual union with her until after Jesus was born, according to Luke, chapter 1 and Matthew 1:25).

While they were there, the time came for her baby to be born. There was no room in the local inn, so she delivered her first baby, a son, in an animals' stable*. She wrapped the boy in strips of cloth, which was the custom of the day, and used a feed trough (a manger) for his bed.

Meanwhile, that night, shepherds sitting out in the fields nearby watching and protecting their sheep. Suddenly, an angel of the Lord appeared to them, and the radiant glory of God shone around them. They were terrified, but the angel said to them, "Do not be afraid, I bring you good news of great joy that will be for all people. Today in the town of David, a Savior has been born to you; He is Christ the Lord! This will be a sign to you: you will find Him wrapped in cloths and lying in a manger."

At that moment, a great company of angels appeared, praising God and saying, "Glory to God in the highest, and on earth peace to men on whom His favor rests."

After the angels left, the shepherds said to each other, "Let's go into Bethlehem and see this thing that has happened, which the Lord has told us about."

So they went into town and found Mary and Joseph and the baby, who was lying in a manger just as the angel had said. After seeing the child, the shepherds spread the news about His coming, and all who heard were amazed at what they told them. Mary treasured these things in her heart and the shepherds returned to work, glorifying and praising God for all they had seen and heard.

*The Bible doesn't actually say Jesus was born in a stable, but it is strongly implied by verse 7, which says "she wrapped Him in cloths and placed Him in a manger, because there was no room for them in the inn." Mangers are feed troughs used in stables. Either Jesus was born in a stable, or He was born in an empty cave or house and someone went out and got a manger out of a stable to use as His bed. Tradition has long held that Jesus was born in a particular cave in Bethlehem and should be weighted accordingly.

Applications

1. Jesus was born into humble circumstances, to humble people.

Jesus could have been born in the nicest hotel or home in the city. But He was born to poor people (we know this based on Joseph's occupation and their sacrifice given in verse 24.), in a small, unexciting town, in a stable. The inn in Bethlehem was probably little more than a house with a couple of extra rooms, but even that was full, so Jesus was born where there was room for Him. *He wasn't pushy then and isn't now.*

Mary and Joseph were very special people. They were not rich or royal, they were humble and obedient. They were morally pure and cared for each other. **Luke 1** and **Matthew 1** tell us the extraordinary circumstances surrounding her becoming pregnant by God Himself and Joseph believing in her word and in God's Word. Joseph could have had her stoned to death in the street for becoming pregnant, but trusted God's promise that the child was conceived supernaturally.

God is looking for morally pure young people who are willing to trust Him in all things. He chooses such people to do mighty things.

God didn't announce the birth of His Son in a big mega church or even the local temple - He told shepherds. The irony here is that shepherds were considered so poor and dirty, they were not allowed into the inner courts of the temple! God did not come just for rich folks, clean folks, or folks with a certain skin color. He came for all people in all circumstances and loves all of us equally. He proved this by announcing the most important birth in history to some of the poorest, dirtiest people in society.

The stable itself was undoubtedly dark and dirty. There was no team of doctors and nurses, electricity, or modern sanitation. These were not the best and cleanest of conditions, but again, Jesus will only go where He is welcomed.

Even the town of Bethlehem was small and uneventful. It was near Jerusalem, where the action was, but far enough away to be small and quiet. Bethlehem was David's home town, though, and **Micah 5:2** said the Messiah would be born there. God brought Joseph and Mary all the way from Nazareth to fulfill that prophecy.

2. Peace had come to all people.

As we have mentioned, Jesus came to bring salvation to everyone who accepts Him, not just the rich or religious. The peace that Jesus brought, that the angels spoke about, was peace with God. Jesus would satisfy God's anger toward sin and would sooth His wrath against sinners. Someone has to pay for our sins; *we* can, or we can allow *Jesus* to (He did so on the cross but we have to *accept* this gift of grace to receive it.) We can pay for our sins by dying and going to hell; Jesus paid for our sins by bleeding and dying on the cross.

Sin is man's way of telling God, "Leave me alone." Hell is God's way of saying, "Okay."

Hebrews 9:22 says there is no forgiveness without the shedding of blood. Jesus reconciled us to God - that is, He made us friends again by satisfying God's anger when He died for our sins. He brought the most important peace ever - peace with God.

Jesus did His part by dying on the cross and coming back to life, now it is up to us to accept this free gift through faith.

The Christmas story is so wonderful because it tells us how Jesus came to earth as a man and laid down His perfect life for us so that we can be right with God again. Jesus didn't just come to the rich or a certain group of people, but to everyone - and that is what is so wonderful about the gospel: It is for everyone.

3. The shepherds spread the good news about Jesus.

Luke spends a lot of time in this story talking about the shepherds. There is some wonderful symbolism here: The shepherds raised lambs, some of which were used for sacrifice in the temple. The angels announced to them that the *Lamb of God* (**John 1:36**) had come, who would once and for all be sacrificed for the sins of mankind.

One of the details Luke gives us is that they "spread the word" about Jesus' birth. These men, who were not considered clean enough to enter the inner courts of the temple, were the first to tell the good news to others.

Some people may think of Jesus only as the baby in the nativity scene. What better time than Christmas to tell others about that baby - how He grew into a sinless man who died and rose again for us. The shepherds told what they had seen and heard and that is what it means to witness: to tell what we have seen or heard.

Students should tell others what they have seen Jesus do in their lives and the truths they have heard about Him. This is good news for all people.

 **Wrap-up.**

The Christmas story is the great news that God came to earth as one of us and became the ultimate sacrifice for all of us. Jesus left the unfathomable riches of heaven to become a man of very humble circumstances. He was born to humble parents in a humble town in a humble place. There was no room in the inn, so He was apparently born in a cattle stable.

The angels appeared to shepherds in the fields nearby. This is wonderfully ironic because of their low status in life. God was showing us that He loves everyone equally and His grace is for everyone. All we have to do is accept His free gift of salvation. God doesn't care about social position or economic status, He cares about all people everywhere.

Since God is concerned about all people, we should be as well. Just as the shepherds told those around them what they had heard and seen, we too should share the good news about Jesus to everyone we meet.

Peace with God has come and His name is Jesus.

P.S. Don't let people tell you Jesus was born as early as 7 B.C. Dionysius Exignus (Dennis the Short), a Ukrainian monk, set the calendar in the sixth century. He had access to the Vatican's Roman records and used Luke's account of the Quirinius census and when Caesar Augustus and King Herod were in power. Jesus was born in 1 B.C. (Dionysius ignored 0 A.D.) He may have been born in the fall of that year because John said He "tabernacled" (dwelt - **John 1:14**) with us, which might mean He was born during the Feast of Tabernacles, between September and October of that year. Also, He was probably *not* born on December 25th because shepherds did not stay outside with their sheep in the winter. December 25th was set as His birthday by Constantine around 320 A.D., apparently to replace a pagan holiday, Saturnalia, which occured on that date.

Optional Activity:

Spend the remainder of your class time planning a Christmas missions project, and then carry it out at the appropriate time.

Divide your students into teams and have them brainstorm ideas they would like to do this Christmas season.

To get them thinking, suggest:

> Plan a play or musical for a local orphanage or children's home.
>> (These tend to book the Christmas season in advance so you may have to plan well ahead for this one.)
>
> Spend a day, or series of days, at a local soup kitchen, cooking, serving and cleaning-up.
>
> Go to a mall and hand out witnessing tracts.
>
> Prepare and hand out food or goody baskets to shut-ins in your area.
>
> Plan a toy drive for local needy kids.
>
> Plan a food drive for local needy families.
>
> Have each student "adopt" an elderly person in your church and give him or her a Christmas card and gift.
>
> Plan a trip to a local nursing home to sing and make crafts with the residents.

John Writes Revelation
Revelation 1

John was the only disciple who had not died for his faith by the nineties, according to church history. He was exiled to the Island of Patmos, sixty miles west of Ephesus, in the Aegean Sea, as punishment for preaching the gospel. Domitian was Caesar in Rome at that time and was persecuting the church for worshiping God and not him.

The book Revelation, John writes, is the revelation of Jesus Christ.

"Blessed is the one who reads the book and who believes what it says," he writes, "The book is from John and from Jesus Christ Himself, who is the faithful witness, the firstborn from the dead and the ruler of kings of the earth; the One who is, who was and who is to come and from His seven-fold Spirit, the Holy Spirit.

"To Him who loves us and has freed us from our sins by His blood, and has made us to be a kingdom and priests to serve His God and Father - to Him be glory and power for ever and ever!"

Look, He is coming with the clouds, and every eye will see Him, even those who pierced Him; and all the peoples of the earth will mourn because of Him.

"I am the Alpha and the Omega," says the Lord God, "who is, and who was and who is to come - the Almighty."

John was filled with the Spirit one Sunday when he heard a voice behind him - a loud voice, like a trumpet. The voice told John to write on a scroll what he saw and to send it to the seven churches in Asia Minor: Ephesus, Smyrna, Pergamum, Thyatira, Sardis, Philadelphia and Laodicea.

John turned to see where the voice was coming from and saw seven golden lampstands. Among them was one *like a son of man* dressed in a robe reaching down to His feet and with a golden sash around His chest. His head and hair were as white as wool or snow, and His eyes were like blazing fire. His feet were like bronze glowing in a furnace and His voice was like the sound of rushing waters. In His right hand, He held seven stars and out of His mouth came a sharp double-edged sword. His face was like the sun shining in all its brilliance.

When John saw Him, he fell at His feet as though dead. Then Jesus placed His right hand on him and said, "Do not be afraid, I am the First and the Last. I am the Living One. I was dead and behold I am alive for ever and ever! I hold the keys to death and Hades.

"Write, therefore, what you have seen, what is now and what will take place later. The mystery of the seven stars in my right hand and of the seven golden lampstands is this: The seven stars are the angels of the seven churches and the seven lampstands are the seven churches themselves."

1. Revelation is meant to encourage all Christians, everywhere.

Many teachers shy away from Revelation because it has difficult passages and requires much study to properly teach, but it is a wonderful book of truth and encouragement and should be taught to all Christians.

John was an older man, living in Ephesus and preaching the gospel when Domitian exiled him to the Island of Patmos in 95 A.D., according to church tradition. John says he was exiled "because of the word of God and the testimony of Jesus". In other words, for preaching the gospel. Scholars say all of the disciples were killed for their faith except John, who was sentenced to live on this small island for about a year and a half.

While on the island, he received this revelation of Jesus. John didn't say it was a revelation (or expose') *about* Jesus, but *of* Jesus - exposing what Jesus wants to say and show.

Jesus instructed John to write in Revelation encouraging words to the church. John admonished it to stand firm during its present and future persecution. Jesus also reminded the churches to love Him first, serve Him only and hate evil.

The seven churches listed in this chapter represent all churches. Seven is the perfect - or complete - number in this type of scripture. This type of writing is called "apocalyptic", which means it uses symbolic imagery to communicate hope for those in the midst of persecution.

2. Jesus is not the humble servant in Revelation that we found in the gospels.

The description we find of Jesus in Revelation is one of a Lord and God of the universe. Jesus was humble and mild in the gospels, but when He returns, He will be riding a white horse with the words "King of Kings and Lord of Lords" on His robe and on His thigh (**Revelation 19:16**). He will come with judgment and power and every knee will bow to Him (**Philippians 2:10-11**). Never again will

He be mistreated or spoken down to. He is God and He will rule forever.

In verses 12 and 13, John turned and saw Jesus standing among the seven lampstands. He describes Him:

He looked like a son of man.

Jesus often referred to Himself as the son of man. This is an allusion to **Daniel 7:13-14**, where Daniel describes the Messiah this way.

Dressed in a robe down to His feet.

Only a priest, prince or a king wore a robe that went down to his feet.

and with a golden sash.

Only a high priest wore a golden sash. John was saying Jesus is a priest who enters into God's holy presence. He is also saying Jesus is a priest and King.

His head and hair were white like wool, as white as snow.

From **Daniel 7:9**, this was Daniel's description of the Ancient of Days - in other words, God Himself. God is pure and older than all of creation. Jesus then, is God.

His eyes were like blazing fire.

From **Daniel 10:6**, the description of God's messenger. Many scholars believe this is also an allusion to the *judgment* Jesus will bring with Him.

His feet were like bronze glowing in a furnace.

Again, a reference to Daniel. **Daniel 10:6**. This may be a reference to speed and strength. Jesus will punish sin and sinners quickly, with power.

His voice was like the sound of rushing waters.

In **Ezekiel 43:2**, this is the description of God's very voice. You can almost hear the power, volume, and roar of a great waterfall in this word picture.

In His right hand He held seven stars.

Jesus is holding the church in His right (strongest) hand. He holds the universal church - all Christians everywhere, and He is holding individual churches in His hand. It is all about Him. The Church belongs to Him and is empowered by Him.

Out of His mouth came a sharp, double-edged sword.

This is the Word of God - the Bible itself. **Hebrews 4:12** describes the Word of God this way. The sword of the Spirit is the only offensive weapon in the armor of God in **Ephesians 6**. God's word pierces to our very hearts. It punishes sin and sets the captives free.

His face was like the sun shining in all its brilliance.

John clearly remembered when Jesus' face "shone like the sun" on the Mount of Transfiguration (**Matthew 17:2**). This is a picture of deity; of the glory of God shining forth. Jesus is powerful, loving, and pure.

3. Although Jesus is a conquering King, He is also our loving Savior.

After John identifies himself as the writer of the book (this is John the disciple) he begins to give us glimpses into the true identity of Christ. We have already considered the description of the *son of man* he saw standing among the lampstands, but he began his accolades much earlier in the chapter.

John gives us a clear picture of the Trinity in verses 4 - 6.

He describes God the Father as Him "who is, and who was, and who is to come." God is the first and the last, the creator of everything, and the final authority.

He calls the Holy Spirit the "seven-fold Spirit before His throne." Clearly, here, he is making reference to the Holy Spirit.

Then, he mentions Jesus Christ, "who is the faithful witness, the firstborn from the dead and the ruler of the kings of the earth." Jesus was faithful to bring us the message of salvation and hope, He is the Lord of both the living and the dead and was the first to be resurrected into His new body. Also, Jesus is the ultimate authority over every king and kingdom.

Jesus loves us and freed us from our sins by His blood, and has made us to be a kingdom of priests to serve God. Because of this, He deserves all praise and glory forever.

He *loves us* (present tense), and *freed us* from our sins with His own blood (past tense). As we have discussed, Jesus was the ultimate sacrifice that satisfied God's wrath toward sin. This sacrifice was done once and for all at the cross (**Hebrews 10:12**). Now we have access to God Himself, something that was reserved only for the high priests - and only once per year - before Calvary. This is why the curtain in the temple split from top to bottom while Jesus was on the cross (**Matthew 27:51**). There is no hierarchy in the Kingdom of God, we are all equal in God's sight. We are all God's priests.

John then says Jesus is coming back soon in the clouds - just as He left us. Everyone will see Him, even those who *pierced* Him (**Zechariah 12:10**).

Jesus is the Alpha and the Omega (the A and the Z, in Greek), the first and the last, the one who is, who was and who is to come, the Almighty. Jesus is I AM.

Wrap-up.

Blessed are those who read Revelation. It is full of words of encouragement for all Christians, everywhere. Jesus instructed John to write it to the Church to encourage Christians to stand firm in the faith during persecution and peace.

Jesus is described as King of Kings and Lord of Lords in Revelation. He is coming back to get His bride, the Church, and He is bringing judgment upon those who reject Him. Jesus is the first and the last. He loves us and freed us from our sins. He will be seen and worshiped by all. He is God. He is Almighty. He is I AM.

Optional Activity:

Divide your students into **seven** teams. Assign each team a church from **Revelation 2** and **3**. Instruct each team to go to a different area or room. Have them elect leaders for each team.

Give them 10 to 15 minutes to prepare a report on their assigned church.

Have them:
1. Tell which church they are studying.
2. Tell what compliments Jesus gave to their church and how it can apply to their church today.
3. Tell what criticisms Jesus had about their church and how it can apply to their church today.
4. Tell what else Jesus said to their church.

After their time is up, assemble them back together and have them make their reports to the other students in the order of the churches in the Bible.